STAINED
GLASS
MARRIAGE

STAINED GLASS MARRIAGE

Hope for Shattered Homes

BY

DALE AND JENA FOREHAND

New Hope Publishers
Birmingham, Alabama

New Hope® Publishers
P. O. Box 12065
Birmingham, AL 35202-2065
www.newhopepubl.com

Library of Congress Cataloging-in-Publication Data

Cover design by Kevin Keller, designconcepts

ISBN: 1-56309-758-3

N034116 • 0403 • 8.5M1

Dedication

To God, the restorer of all good things. To our parents, Jack and Sandra Sadler and Sherman and Gloria Forehand, thank you for being our *paracletes* through the tough times. To our extended family for standing in the gap for us both. To Lynn and Debbie Bullock, for your endless encouragement, friendship, and accountability through life and the writing of this book. To Kelly Cousins, for letting yourself be used of God to help us heal our marriage. To all the churches that opened your hearts and homes to our ministry. And most of all, to our children, Cole and Jorja. You are our heroes for your courage and comeback from a devastating experience.

Table of Contents

Introduction

Each one of us has a story. Our stories may involve different characters and circumstances, but all have one com-
monality: they all involve a journey. This journey is
definitely taking us somewhere. We do, however, get to
play a part in choosing where the journey ends.

The story you will be reading is our journey. It's a story
about the death, burial, and resurrection of our marriage.
But this story is not just about us. It is about hope. For as
long as we have Jesus, we have hope. This is also a story
about what God can do when He is allowed to invade the
lives of people. Our marriage was saved by the pure grace
of God. He gave us a broken spirit and a desire to turn
from our selfish ways and completely trust Him in obedience.
Out of our willingness to trust and obey, God took us on
a journey to wholeness. We found that only when we, as
individuals, became whole could our marriage relationship
become healthy and whole, bringing glory to God. Then
our house became a home where He reigned as Lord.

Perhaps you are reading this book because you have
a good marriage, but want it to be better. Perhaps your
marriage is not what it should be. You may even have a
marriage that is struggling to survive. Maybe you are

divorced, and feel devastated and alone. Whatever your circumstances, we encourage you to walk with us on a road less traveled. God can take the broken pieces of your life and put them back together again.

We have designed this book for individuals who desire to grow in their relationship with Christ, thus affecting their relationship with their spouse. This book is by no means a quick fix that guarantees your story will have our same ending. That depends on you, your spouse, and your obedience to the Spirit's call on your life. We do guarantee, however, that God's Word is true, that He is faithful, and that He can bring healing through His awesome power and grace.

Too many times in our lives, we have started reading a book with the best of intentions to complete it, but we never make it through. We encourage you to read this book in its entirety so that you can grasp the full intent of this book and hear God's truths throughout. This book should not replace your daily communion with God. This is intended to enhance your walk, as an addition to your daily devotion and prayer time.

We want you to begin to prepare your hearts for your time with God as you read the pages that follow. Let us offer you just a few suggestions:

• **Ask the Holy Spirit to reveal to you areas in *your* life that need to be crucified.** This book is not for you to think about how your spouse needs to hear this! This is a special time of communion with you and God, dealing with you and you alone (Psalm 139:23).

• **Ask the Lord to make your heart tender toward His truth and then give you the strength to walk in obedience to His truths.** Personal evaluation will allow you to check the condition of your heart as you read from day to day (John 8:32).

• **Ask the Comforter to comfort you as you visit places in your journey, so that you can best encourage someone else through your life.** As God begins to mold and shape you into His image, you will be able to take your life's experiences, and the things the Holy Spirit has taught you as you read, and help minister to other sojourners along the way. The fact is that we learn from one another and thus should share with one another what the Holy Spirit has revealed to us (2 Corinthians 1:3–4).

• **Ask God to make Himself highly exalted in your life and draw you nearer to Him.** If you want to get the most from this book, you must be willing to let God go to the very depths of your soul and do His healing work (James 4:8).

Are you ready to join us on this journey? We are thrilled that God has divinely appointed this time for us. He is so ready to meet us wherever we are, and take us, moment by moment, to where He wants us to be. As you read our story, know that God has a story to make of your life and marriage. As He does His awesome work—molding, breaking, and crafting you into His image—don't give up. Stay the course. Our relationships with other people and, most importantly, our relationship with Christ will never be the same as we discipline ourselves and yield ourselves to His leadership. Let the journey begin!

Chapter One

Broken Pieces

I n 1996, our marriage had reached an all-time low. There was no love, no joy, no relationship. Misplaced priorities and neglect had delivered us to the doorway of divorce. Dale and I (Jena) were both extremely active in church. We brought two precious children into the world, Cole and Jorja. We had built a nice house and lived in a nice part of town. Dale was a new deacon in the church. I was a leading soloist and had just finished writing an Easter musical for the church choir. Together we taught a young married Sunday school class. From the outside looking in, we seemed to have the perfect marriage, the perfect life. In reality, both of us were *doing life* while neglecting the marriage that once took priority.

After years of carelessness, complacency, selfishness, and total disregard for the other, a marriage that once bore beautiful fruit was withering on the vine. We suppressed our emotional pain, which had developed into a bitter cancer that had turned love to hate, freedom to bondage. The wounds we inflicted on each other's heart left us bleeding to death with no hope for recovery. The pain was so intense that we believed the only way to survive was to get out.

The Marriage Shatters

On a Saturday in July of 1996, Dale walked into our home and took my suitcases out from under our bed and began to pack my clothes. He said that the marriage was over. He told me to get out of his house because he was finished with the relationship. I followed Dale into the bathroom as he packed my things. Dale closed the bathroom door behind me, held it shut, and began to hurl verbal attacks. Our son Cole was banging on the door, begging to get inside. When I attempted to leave, Dale held the door strongly and laughed as I struggled to get out.

Dale grabbed our children, Cole (age 5) and Jorja (18 months) and loaded them into his car. As I stood sobbing in the driveway, I could not believe what our marriage had become. Dale sped off with the children and headed for the golf course. Playing golf was a release for him where he could get away from the problems at hand. He left the children with his mother at the swimming pool. I reached the pool, gathered the children, and headed to my sister's house to stay for a period of time for things to cool off. When Dale realized what I had done while he played golf, he became incredibly angry. I called Dale and explained that I was afraid of him and wanted to stay away for a while until I felt safe again.

Internal frustrations and lack of control angered Dale. He became so enraged that he began to verbally attack and threaten me. He demanded that I return the children. Thus, I became even more afraid for me and Cole and Jorja. After four days, I met Dale at a park so the children could play and visit with him. There was no conversation between the two of us, and the tension was thick.

I did not know that Dale had gone to see a lawyer. The lawyer made this statement to Dale: "Those kids are just as much yours as they are hers. If I were you, I'd go and get them." For a guy with anger and control problems, this sounded like a great plan.

The next week was Vacation Bible School at our church. I had responsibilities there, so I brought the children and participated as if nothing had happened. While I was cleaning up at the conclusion of the day, Cole was playing in the gymnasium and Jorja was with me at the entrance. Dale drove to the front of the gym, determined to get our children. I saw him and quickly ran into the gym to get Cole. As I sat Jorja on the ground and yelled for Cole to come to me, I turned around to see Dale grabbing Jorja and scrambling to the car. Cole jumped into my arms and began asking me what was happening and why his daddy was taking Jorja. Panicking, I repeatedly whispered in Cole's ear that it was all going to be okay. With Cole in my arms, I chased Dale to his car. He drove away.

I then went back into the gymnasium, and there I met Dale's twin brother, Dave. He pulled Cole out of my arms, knocking me to the ground as I fought to hang on to my child. As Dave ran with Cole to the car that waited outside, Cole screamed out for me in hysteria. As I sat on the gym floor, Cole's voiced echoed, "Mommy! Mommy! I want my mommy!" And then there was nothing, nothing but silence.

I sat confused and in shock at what had just taken place. Though people quickly made themselves scarce, a few helped me to my feet and encouraged me to call the police. As my family arrived to help, I began reporting the incident to a policeman who had arrived on the scene. As he wrote the report, he explained that Dale was the father and there was nothing he could do about him taking them. The best advice he could give was to call an attorney.

Meanwhile, Dale went to his parents' house, packed some bags, loaded them into his car, and disappeared with the children for seven days. They went to the U.S. Space and Rocket Center in Huntsville, Alabama. They traveled to Chattanooga, Tennessee, to peer through the big glass and see all the fish at the aquarium. For seven days, Dale ran from our problems while I lay in a small dark bedroom in my sister's home, destitute, scared, and alone.

After fruitless attempts to locate the children, I picked up the phone and made a call to an attorney, something I never dreamed of doing. During my first visit, I was advised that the only way to get my children back into the state of Alabama was to file for a divorce. The attorney drew up the papers and an officer was sent to serve them to Dale.

On the back roads of a Tennessee highway, Dale's cell phone rang. It was his employer telling him that they had just received papers that read, "Forehand versus Forehand." Dale's heart fell to the depths of his soul as we both realized that we were about to face the most excruciating process we had ever experienced . . . divorce.

Upon my arrival at the courthouse, I was told that it would be a long process unless Dale and I could negotiate with each other with the aid of our lawyers. We both wanted full custody, however, and both refused to leave the marital residence. That left the judge with no choice but to place us back in the house together pending a divorce trial.

In-House Prison

For 15 months we lived in the house together, awaiting the trial date. The house that used to be a home had now become a prison. Dale took the master bedroom and locked me out to find my own place to sleep. I went down the hall and locked myself in Cole's bedroom. I slept with him in his red wrought-iron bunk beds. Many nights I cried myself to sleep while our six-year-old son, Cole, patted me sweetly on the back.

As time moved on, we journeyed back to court on several occasions, each accusing the other of breaking the rules. The judge ruled that we must have the children in the residence by six P.M. every night because of our game-playing, manipulation, and deceit. Being bound to a curfew forced us to spend time together, and our house seemed to get smaller with each passing day.

Because of Dale's anger and desire for control, he withheld all our money from me. Being a stay-at-home mother, I was reduced to begging from Dale or borrowing from friends and family, a very humbling and shaming experience. Dale would give me a credit card, but one false move and he ripped it away. This push and pull between us was evidence that our marriage had completely disintegrated.

We began conducting ourselves as if the other did not exist. We locked doors, separated our clothes and food, and pulled our children from one parent to the other as we each tried to win their love. When we did engage in conversation, our talks escalated into full-fledged arguments that left us wounded and cold. Many fights became so heated that Cole would sit in the corner of the dining room and cry with his hands over his ears, begging for it to stop. We threw things, pointed our fingers, and verbally abused one another.

We tried to buy our children's love with gifts. We made plans to keep the other from seeing the children. Manipulation became a learned behavior, and we showed no conscience in the process. The children quickly learned to manipulate as well. There were many situations where they would work the circumstances to force us to be at odds with each other and thus get their own way.

Christmas was a gut-wrenching experience. Splitting time with the children over the holidays was a mess; the lawyers made another trip to the judge because we could not agree on any terms. We could not even agree on a time to go and get a Christmas tree together for the house. So the children and I got one tree and placed it in the den, and Dale took the children and purchased another tree for the dining room.

I had no money to buy gifts for the children, and there was no way that Dale would give me any money to spend on them. I had no hope that I would be able to give my children anything for Christmas. One afternoon, a friend called me. She picked me up and took me to Wal-mart and purchased the children Christmas gifts for me to give them. I stood in the checkout line and cried as the reality of my life began to strike to the core of my being.

Christmas Eve finally came. I came out of the bedroom first and placed my "Santa" gifts out in the den floor. After I went back to my bedroom and locked my door, Dale was now free to come and display his part of "Santa." The next morning was a smothering event as both of us put on our happy faces and pretended to be a family.

Things continued to unravel as two lawyers (who each wanted his client to win) spent time coaching us in the ways of mischief. We paid private investigators. We wore tape recorders to catch the other in some incriminating conversation. We tapped phones and kept perfect records to build our own cases. We provoked the other to anger so we could accuse each other of misconduct. Our house had become a war zone, and the casualties of that war were not only two adults but also two beautiful children.

After we had lived in this hell for fifteen months, my lawyer informed me that we would finally get our day in court. The date was set, my lawyer was prepared, and a glimmer of hope that all of this might be over soon was in sight.

The Court Decrees

When our time came up on the docket, I was led into a small courtroom with my lawyer at my side. Dale and I each entered the room carrying a box that represented our lives. As the judge entered and took his place, we rose in honor of his position. The hammer of the gavel meant only one thing . . . the battle lines were drawn, and the war was about to be waged.

The next four days were spent listening to family member after family member and friend after friend testify from the witness stand. They had chosen sides, and their goal was to convince the judge what a terrible parent one of us was, thus influencing who should gain custody of our children. Lies and deceit filled the courtroom. Our parents, who once loved their child's spouse, were now doing all that they could to take care of their own flesh and blood. And with every comment came a stab of emotional pain that penetrated to the very depths of the soul. During those four days of trial, it felt as if our lives were being ripped into shreds and then being placed into our hands. Four days came and went, and as the gavel fell for the last time, we left the courthouse with our arms full of life's broken pieces.

We were told to go back into the house together pending the results of the trial. Those four weeks that followed felt as if I was smothering, awaiting the outcome that would forever change my life. We finally received the papers, the divorce was final, and joint custody was awarded.

Hallelujah, it was finally over . . . or was it? My depression and anger seemed to be even more prevalent than ever before. As my emotions swung from the elation of finality to the frustration of always having to communicate with Dale about matters with the children, I found myself on an emotional roller coaster. Yes, the marriage was over, but life continued. The struggles for personal agendas, strategic plans, and the fighting for individual time with the children began to escalate even more. We had to discuss everything pertaining to our children before we could make a decision. And every other weekend as we passed the children to the other, we felt as if our own hearts were physically being ripped apart. The anger, frustration, and pain were indescribable.

Divorce . . . it's a forever funeral as a part of you dies every other weekend, while your child grips your neck and begs you not to leave. Divorce . . . it is what I thought I wanted, and yet I was more miserable than I had ever been before. Divorce . . . it affects you physically, emotionally, and spiritually. All that is left is a shattered reflection of what used to be. And the pain associated cannot be compared to anything except a grievous death.

Stained Glass Marriage

The above is the story of the death of our marriage. And all too often, it is the story of so many others. In our case, the story didn't end there. God did not look down from the glory of heaven and say "Dale and Jena, you have messed things up so badly that I can't fix it anymore." Instead, He graciously said, "I'll wipe this clean and help you start over if you will let Me." Two very broken people, not knowing what the other was doing, both dragged themselves to the foot of the cross and fell at their Savior's feet and begged for His forgiveness and help.

One Wednesday morning, four weeks after the final verdict, I called Dale to discuss some gymnastics arrangements for Jorja. Dale, still hanging on to the anger from the battle, told me that he would not be taking Jorja anywhere when she was with him, and yet another argument began to brew. Our yelling got so intense that Dale had to close his office door to muffle the sound.

In the middle of this heightened argument, I let Dale see the truth within my heart for just a moment. We call this a "window of opportunity." This window occurs when we allow someone to see the purest form of who we are from the depths of our hearts without reservations or hidden agendas. The heart is laying out there, exposed, naked, and bare. Our children do this when they reveal the very deepest parts of their hearts. For instance, once Cole was in his bed at night and shared that he got called a "sissy" at school because he couldn't do as many pull-ups as the next kid. Many times we don't receive and embrace this window of opportunity, but make light of it. We say things like, "Grow up! Get over it!" leaving our children alone and misunderstood. This causes our children to begin building walls of protection around their hearts to protect them from the hurt that they experienced. And if it goes unattended for too long, a day arrives when we can't talk to them at all because they no longer let us in to see their hearts anymore.

I chose to reveal myself that day so that Dale could briefly peek into my heart. It was the scariest thing I had ever done, but God was pushing me forward to obey His prompting. These words began to flow from my heart in the middle of this downwardly-spiraling conversation: "Dale, what have we done? Why don't you just come get me, and let's fix this thing." Like a bolt of lightning, Dale heard words that shocked him to the bone.

Instantly, Dale was faced with a choice to make for himself. Would he respond with fear, pride, or anger? Or would he return my tenderness of heart with the truth of his own? Dale responded with this simple statement: "I can't look at the feet of our children without seeing you." That statement was like a bouquet of roses to me. I didn't think he cared about what I looked like, much less my feet. The Spirit of the Lord began at that very moment to melt the hardened mess of our hearts. The pride, anger, bitterness, resentment, and sheer hatred began to peel back one layer at a time. Within minutes, Dale and I were pouring our hearts out while sobbing uncontrollably.

Dale drove to the house where I was staying. He knocked on the door, and a friend of mine who had testified against him in court answered the door. With great shock and fear on her face, she called for me to come outside. Dale spoke these words from his heart: "Jena, I don't know what all of this means, but I know it is the right thing to do." He kissed me on the cheek and drove away.

We spent the next four months in frequent, intentional marriage counseling with a godly Christian counselor who walked us through the healing process. There were hard days when it seemed like we tap-danced on the painful places where we had sworn never to return. Some days seemed like all was fresh and new, while others made us question our decision to return to each other. At the end of our four months, there was no question in either of our minds that re-marriage was what God wanted from us. So, on December 21, 1997, we were remarried to the glory of God.

On the morning of our re-marriage, Cole entered our bedroom and said, "Since you two are getting together with each other, I think I would like to get together with God." At the foot of our bed, our son prayed with us to receive Jesus as His Savior. Ephesians 3:20 (NKJV) says, "Now to Him who is able to do exceedingly abundantly above all that we ask or think . . . ." God, in His divine plan, not only brought our marriage back together but redeemed our precious child into His family. His plans truly are greater than we could have ever imagined.

Chapter Two

Safety in Marriage

O nce God restored our marriage, many people asked us how our relationship could possibly work after all that had happened. Two recurring questions emerged: "How did you get the love to come back?" and "How did you move past all of the hurt and pain you caused each other?" The chapters to follow will lay before you the journey that brought hope and healing to our shattered home. Our prayer is that you will understand that God does work all things together for good to them that love the Lord and are called according to His purposes (Romans 8:28).

Our first step toward reconciliation was to seek Christian counseling. As we began putting the pieces of our marriage back together, our brokenness brought us face-to-face with our fears. We were afraid to be hurt again. We were afraid to hurt our children. We were afraid of what our friends might think. We were afraid of what the future might hold. And we were afraid of failing. When fear and failure enter a relationship, both parties emotionally shut down. They begin building walls around their hearts that are often hard to break through. A stagnant, non-emotional relationship evolves, in which true intimacy is too distant to fathom.

We were reminded that God's Word tells us in 2 Timothy 1:7, "For God did not give us a spirit of timidity (fear), but a spirit of power, of love and of self-discipline." Thus we pressed forward, leaning on His strength for what was to come.

As our counseling sessions approached their conclusion, nearing the day of our re-marriage, our counselor asked us to do something that revolutionized our understanding of our relationship. She asked us to sit knee to knee and hold hands. She told us to confess the sin that we had allowed in our lives that led to the destruction and death of our marriage. We sat there, looking into each other's eyes, feeling incredibly uncomfortable. Our sweaty palms and pounding hearts indicated we were going to a place we did not want to go.

The knee-to-knee session still stings to the very core, as we remember what our relationship had become. We sat squirming in our seats, not wanting to face each other or the sin in our lives. Our counselor asked Jena, "What's wrong?" Her reply is one that will forever convict. "Over the course of our marriage, I have repeatedly taken my heart out and placed it in Dale's hands only to have him squeeze the life out of it. I am so *afraid* to take my heart out again and place it in his hands, because I don't think I can survive another squeeze." Instantly, we were knee-to-knee and face-to-face with what we had become. The conviction of this truth forever changed us. The sword of Jena's statement thrust us into the reality that our relationship was no longer an emotionally safe place for either of us.

Safe at Home

Safety must be the foundation for every marriage. The enemy wants to hold us captive to our fear, keeping us locked up in our selfishness and self-protection. Why? To make us ineffective ministers to each other. Many times, we attempted to share ourselves with one another only to be rejected, ridiculed, or made to feel small. We make attempts to let our spouse see through the window of our heart, but if met with the same reactions, we withdraw in order to protect ourselves from further hurt. During our first marriage, there were many times Jena felt closer to her friends than to me (Dale). Why? Because she felt *safe* with them, and not with me.

We are not speaking of physical safety, but rather an emotional safety where hearts can be laid bare before the other with complete confidence and trust. If valuables are placed in a safety deposit box, then they are kept from harm, protected, and safe. When a baseball player slides into home base and the umpire yells "Safe!" the player has made it home, safe and sound. He's not out. A marriage that demonstrates safety is one where hearts are protected from harm, naked and not ashamed, where husband and wife have confidence that they are not *out*, but are home, safe and sound.

To understand emotional safety and to be a *safe mate*, we must begin by applying this one truth: **all of our ultimate safety is found first and foremost in the person of Jesus Christ.** Proverbs 18:10 says, "The name of the LORD is a strong tower; the righteous run to it and are safe." Isn't it wonderful to know that we can run to our Savior for our safety? We don't have to trust our fickle feelings, but we are safe and secure from the evil one in the wisdom and protection Christ offers. We can go to the Heavenly Father with everything. He really is the safe tower to which we can run. As we grow in our understanding of the "safe tower" character of God, we then can exemplify these characteristics in our marriages.

Making a Marriage Safe

First, we must be *available* for one another! As we reflected on our relationship, there were many times when we were in the same room yet miles apart emotionally. You may understand exactly what we're talking about. During those moments together, you talk about your day knowing the entire time that your spouse couldn't repeat a word you said! To prove the point, you could say something like, "and then my eyeball fell out" only to hear, "Oh, that's good, honey!" Been there? You might as well have been talking to a wall!

One evening, while Dale was watching TV, I (Jena) wanted to talk with him. Though he appeared to listen, I noticed Dale was more interested in the baseball game than the conversation. Now I have some real stinky feet. So to get Dale's attention, I gently took my shoes off and placed them under his nose. Boy, did that get his attention. Being in close proximity to someone does not necessarily mean they are available to you.

Webster defines *available* as "present and ready for immediate use; willing to do something." As part of our re-marriage celebration, we took our children, Cole and Jorja, to Disney World. During our visit, we had a character lunch with Winnie the Pooh at the Crystal Palace. As we waited for our table, the hostess soon came to us and said, "Forehand, party of four, your table is now available." Did that mean that when we got to the table it was dirty, used, and a mess? No! The table was ready to receive and serve us. In marriage we may be present, but not always ready to receive and serve one another. Being available is more than just being present bodily. It is being ready and willing to do whatever is needed, whether it's listening, advising, encouraging, or understanding. **When we truly die to our own selfish desires and embrace another's needs by being available to them, we are being safe mates.**

Christ stands ready and willing whenever we come to Him in need. Revelation 3:20 says, "Here I am! I stand at the door and knock. If anyone hears my voice and opens the door, I will come in and eat with him, and he with me." We can feel so secure when we understand His wonderful availability toward us. When we make ourselves available in marriage, we are following the safe tower character of our Savior.

Second, we must be *approachable* for one another! Have you ever been afraid to approach someone? Maybe they don't have a welcoming demeanor, or their body language or attitude is threatening. Perhaps in the past, you've had problems dealing with them. Or maybe they've snapped at you during previous conversations, leaving you tempted to ask, "Have you seen the piece of my head you just bit off?" Whatever the circumstances, part of being safe with others is the ability to be approachable.

This occurred for us when I (Dale) would come home from work. I'd walk in the house only to find Jena preoccupied with preparing supper, bathing kids, and finishing homework. She wouldn't even notice that I'd come home! I wouldn't dare approach Jena then—she was concerned about everything else but me. The busy-ness of life can be a major deterrent to emotional safety.

Other times, we become unapproachable to guard ourselves from being manipulated or shamed. Have you ever been approached by someone whose sole motive is to get something from you, or to criticize you? Then you have probably conditioned yourself to be unapproachable. We don't want to face our own inadequacies and imperfections. Therefore in moments of conflict or even simple discussion, we immediately put our defenses up. The other person withdraws in response, and the two people become islands unto themselves.

If someone were to approach you and firmly step on your foot, you might accept his or her apology and not think about it ever again. But if every time you see this person they continually stomp on your foot, you will eventually stay out of their path or wear a steel-toed boot! This is exactly what happens in relationships. If your heart is continually being stomped on, you will eventually remove yourself emotionally, or build some walls around your heart that are extremely difficult to break down.

Consider for a moment the Old Testament duties of the high priest. The old covenant required the high priest to crawl under the veil and offer sacrifices for the atonement of the people's sins. Only the high priest was allowed in the Holy of Holies, the most sacred place before God. As the high priest entered under the veil, a rope was tied to his ankle. This was so that, if he were struck dead because of his own un-cleanness or failure to complete his duties properly, temple servants could drag him out from under the veil and send another priest in his stead. Does that sound like an approachable and safe place to you?

But when Jesus Christ came, fully available, and gave Himself as our High Priest, once and for all, the veil of the temple was rent from top to bottom. God's Word says that now all of us can boldly *approach* the throne of grace and receive mercy (Hebrews 4:16). Ephesians 3:12 says, "In him and through faith in him we may *approach* God with freedom and confidence." Now that sounds like safety to us! We are totally welcome to approach God through Jesus at any time, any place, with any thing.

How do we usually welcome children? We bend down and stretch out our arms wide to welcome them with a big hug. They run into our open arms, almost knocking us over with delight, while we hold them tightly and lovingly. Mark 9:36–37 says, "He took a little child and had him stand among them. Taking him in his arms, he said to them, 'Whoever welcomes one of these little children in my name welcomes me.'" Can you imagine, for just a moment, how incredible it would be to have Jesus hold His outstretched arms for you? He did just that more than 2000 years ago on a tree at Calvary. His arms are still open today to anyone who will run to Him.

Being a safe mate means that you welcome your spouse with open arms. It means that they do not have to be fearful about coming to you with an open heart. Can that be said of you? If you have not been approachable in the past, the time is now to confess and seek forgiveness. If you practice approachability with God and your spouse, it will be evident by the intimacy that grows in these relationships. Welcome others into conversation and fellowship with outstretched arms. God will take care of the rest.

Third, we must be *accepting* of our mate. There are times when we may have made ourselves available and approachable, but we haven't been *accepting* of what our mate shares with us. The battleground of an unhealthy marriage has led to criticism and shared hurt. All our mate tells us is what we're doing wrong and how we've hurt them. Our first response, then, is to become defensive. After all, who do they think they are, making such accusations? They need to "control their emotions," "stop being so sensitive," and "just get over it!" Ever said those words? Ever heard those words? Remarks like these can be definite safety-busters.

When you are accepting of your mate, you listen, receive, evaluate, and *then* respond to what you have heard. In many circumstances, we are guilty of listening only partially, and then responding, without receiving and evaluating what was shared. We quickly jump to the defense, especially when we feel we're being blamed. Turning a deaf ear to the rest of your spouse's words, you quickly think of everything you can say that will give you leverage or help you to win the battle. **The truth is that your spouse is not your enemy.** There is no need to jump to the defense, especially without first completely hearing what your spouse is trying to say.

When you have a safe marriage, you will accept what your spouse shares, encouraging them to speak freely, without fear of your response. Yet if you or your spouse has responded with harshness, you can be sure that acceptable safety has been damaged.

There is a healthier way to be accepting, when our husband or wife approaches us. One of the things that endeared Jena to me (Dale) was her outgoing, bubbly, people-loving personality. During the early years of our marriage, we often got together with friends, playing cards and games, and going to sporting events. Over time, I felt that Jena was spending more of her time and attention with our friends than with me. The qualities that I was first attracted to became a source of irritation. In order to get some of my own attention, I would make her the butt of my jokes, even if it was hurtful toward her. Later, Jena would try to tell me how she felt. "Tonight when you made me the butt of your jokes, that really hurt my feelings." But I responded, "Give me a break! It was just a joke! Get over it!" I did not want to accept what Jena had to share.

When this happens in marriage, no one benefits from the conversation. I should have responded to Jena, "You know, I didn't mean to embarrass you. I guess I just wanted to be funny, but that was wrong for me to do that at your expense. I'm sorry. Will you forgive me?" Accepting what your spouse shares (and responsibility for hurtful actions or words) promotes growth and healing. That strengthens a relationship. Both need to be aware of an action that hurts the other. God can use that to bring you closer to each other as you avoid hurting your mate in the future. Allow the Spirit of God to mold you into His image and rid you of things in your life that are not pleasing to Him. Friend, this is where our world (and our mates) will begin to see a difference in us.

Jesus is the perfect example for us to follow. God knew we would need not only His Word, but also someone in bodily form to show us how to put His guidance into practice. And so the Word became flesh, in the person of Jesus. In John 4, we find a conversation between Jesus and the woman at the well. Have you ever noticed how Christ made Himself available and approachable to her? He accepted her questioning of Him, and He responded to her in a loving way that let her know that He was different. His words caused her heart to soften, and changed her response toward Him. If safety is to become certain in your marriage, you must follow Christ's example.

Being *accountable* is the fourth element of being a safe mate. We have made ourselves available, approachable, and acceptable. Now it's time to develop a healthy accountability. Most of us are willing to hold other people accountable, but we don't want to be accountable to anyone else.

Pride is often the culprit, as well as years of worldly conditioning of our hearts. For instance, Dale, like so many men, doesn't like to ask for directions. Anytime we get lost, it seems as though a supernatural infusion of "macho-testosterone" keeps him from asking, "Can someone help me here?" Too many times this is true of our life's relationships as well. When we get lost in our relationships, we have too much pride to ask for help. We shudder at the thought of placing our hearts out there, acknowledging our need for help. Accountability is a crucial principle found in a safe marriage. In reality, life is hard, temptation is everywhere, and sin is real. We all need people in our lives who can help us along the way. God, by His divine plan, created the marriage relationship to be so safe and such a strong tower of support that intimate accountability between a husband and a wife is welcomed and not rejected.

The problem with accountability is that few people understand the rewards involved. We don't ask for accountability because we are afraid we will have to answer to someone for our failures, just as we would have to admit our "lost-ness" to the person giving us directions. True accountability requires letting someone else into the deepest part of our lives. When accountability takes place, the rewards are significant. You no longer travel your journey alone.

However, accountability can be abused when we hold people accountable for things that they have not asked us to hold them accountable for. They may not be ready for the accountability, and our responses seem more like judgment and condemnation to them. People then develop resistance and feelings of resentment.

Jena's doctor encourages her to drink a lot of water. If she shares that with me (Dale), but I minimize the advice and make her feel stupid for even talking to me about it, there is no support or accountability. Now consider this: We go to a restaurant and Jena orders a Dr. Pepper. I say to the waiter, "No, she'll have water." You can bet Jena will be resentful of me telling her what to do! But if Jena asks me to hold her accountable for drinking more water, and I have been available, approachable, and accepting of her, I can respond to her at the restaurant, "Don't you think you might drink water? You know it would be better for you." Then we've avoided damaged feelings and strengthened our relationship.

Proverbs 27:17 says, "As iron sharpens iron, so one man sharpens another." It's imperative we learn that accountability must be coupled with tenderness, comfort, love, affirmation, encouragement, and example. God gives us specific guidelines for accountability. The Bible addresses this in 1 Corinthians 4:21: "What do you prefer? Shall I come to you with a whip, or in love and with a gentle spirit?" In a safe marriage, accountability can yield the peaceful fruit of righteousness, offering healing to all who embrace it (Hebrews 12:11–13). If your marriage is not safe, then accountability for you will be an exercise in judgment and condemnation. Only when availability, approachability, and acceptance have been established can accountability be received as concern and constructive encouragement.

Finally, in a safe marriage, both partners are able to be vulnerable. Once the previous four elements of safety have been firmly established, the last quality will be exemplified without any hidden agendas or personal reservations. Vulnerability is the "no strings attached" element of being a safe mate. True vulnerability happens when you reveal yourself deeply, legitimately desiring a loving response, but never demanding one.

Has someone ever bared their soul to you, seeking a particular response to their unspoken purpose? For example, has your mate ever come into the house and been very kind and talkative and touchy toward you unexpectedly? Soon you realize what they really want. The holy huddle! SEX!

And if it does not happen, your spouse may pout or not even speak to you for a couple of days! Sadly, this scenario is happening in too many marriages. Many believe that vulnerability is sex. Sex may be a part of vulnerability, but there is much more to it.

Couples believe they are being vulnerable in marriage simply by sharing something to get a response. This is not vulnerability, but rather manipulation. When manipulation is the standard operating procedure, then a spouse feels more like an object, and not a soulmate. The physical connection of sex seems more like a duty and not a desire to have the intimate, heart-connected, body-connected relationship that God intended. How do you know whether you are being vulnerable or manipulative? The example above would pass the true test for vulnerability if the holy huddle didn't happen and no one got upset over it! Relationships suffer when demand overtakes desire.

Vulnerability is the opening up of your heart to another, revealing your hopes, your dreams, your feelings, your passions, your failures, and your struggles to one another. While many of us would desire to have a marriage relationship that was full of vulnerability and intimacy, many of us never reach this pinnacle. Why? Because true vulnerability is scary. It forces you to reveal the deepest parts of yourself to another who has the power to embrace it or reject it. With vulnerability comes a challenge for us to hold gently the hearts of our spouses and others. When you have a level of confidence and trust that allows you to speak freely about the deep recesses of your heart, then you are quickly achieving safety in your relationship.

Taking a long, deliberate look at the life of Christ, you cannot help but see what a safe person He was then, and is even now as you read. He is always available. He is always approachable. He is wholly accepting of us. He holds us accountable by His Word, and the convicting power of the Holy Spirit. And He was vulnerable, all the way to the cross.

Regaining Emotional Safety

When emotional safety is lost in your marriage, you can find it once again by becoming a safe mate. The five elements of safety work in a cycle to maintain a safe environment for a growing relationship. As we make ourselves available and approachable, we begin to receive healthy communication from our spouses. As they positively accept us and our comments, we can move into accountability and vulnerability. As we begin to see the development of openness, we become more available and approachable. And the cycle continues.

If you feel your marriage has been shattered, you can probably remember a time that was like our knee-to-knee session—you could no longer open your hearts to each other. You were no longer (or had never been) safe mates. If you have realized a lack of emotional safety in your marriage, there is hope for you. Safety can be regained if both parties are willing.

For Jena and me (Dale), safety began to return when we shared our fears with one another. When Jena shared, "Over the course of our marriage, I have repeatedly taken my heart out and placed it in Dale's hands only to have him squeeze the life out of it. I am so afraid to place my heart in his hands again, because I don't think I can survive another squeeze," I got on my knees crying and replied, "Jena, if you will give me one more chance, I commit to never squeeze your heart again." It broke down the walls we'd built around our hearts. We both committed to take our hearts out one more time, give each other one more chance, trying never to squeeze each other's heart again. Our God is a God of second chances. We encourage you to be a person who will give safety one more chance. Our firsthand experience is that God will honor your efforts and obedience.

We have purposely designated this initial chapter toward your understanding of safety and the safe tower character of Christ. The depth of growth that can result for you as an individual and for your relationship with one another is contingent upon the safety found in an intimate personal relationship with Christ. Out of the overflow of that relationship, God, by His divine wisdom and power, will enable you to become a safe mate.

Our prayer is that through the remaining chapters in this book, you will accept the challenge to practice safety. Christ is the safest person there is. Run to His safe tower, then take that safety into your marriage. You will experience a deeper walk with God and your relationship with your spouse will thrive. Both can become a beautiful testimony of the goodness and grace of our Lord. Hang in there! We still have much to discover on our journey together.

Chapter Three

Marital Bliss
or Marital Bust

We met a couple not too long ago who had only been married two weeks. They were "goo-goo-ing" at each other continually. "Pumpkin" was their perpetual name for each other. They believed they had the perfect marriage and that the world was a wonderful place because of all the happiness they felt. They had big aspirations for their future together, and life was grand.

Meet Adam and Eve. Their new marriage was the ultimate, utopian honeymoon in the Garden of Eden. They have the perfect marriage in the perfect place. Adam is the king and Eve is his queen and they are complete, content, and happy. We call this utopian scenario "marital bliss."

Marital Bliss

We all want it. We dreamed of it before marriage, and thought we would achieve it when we married our spouse.

The problem was, and remains today, that we've never known what marital bliss really looks like, or how to get it. We've tried a myriad of methods only to come up empty-handed. But the Word of God has help for us. Through strategic study in the book of Genesis, we have identified what we believe to be three benchmarks of marital bliss for which all relationships should strive.

Perfection. As we begin reading in Genesis 2, we find that the Garden of Eden was a place of perfection. This garden had anything and everything Adam and Eve needed. Their physical needs were completely satisfied. Their emotional needs were completely fulfilled. And God was the complete supplier of it all. They were even in perfect relationship with their Heavenly Father (the Creator), as He walked with them in the cool of the day. It was a perfect marriage, in perfect bliss, in a perfect place.

Do any of us know any perfect marriages today? NO! There are no perfect marriages. But does that mean that we are not to strive for perfection? Just as Paul says in Romans 6:1–2, do we continue in sin because of the abundance of grace freely given? The answer to both is "God forbid!" We must be ever striving for perfection in our marriages. We will not reach perfection until our glorification, but until then, we must press on toward that goal (Philippians 3:14). If you strive for perfection, you might obtain excellence along the way.

We don't have to be a perfect person to attain a perfect marriage, for there is no such person and no such thing.

But rather the perfect Savior, Jesus Christ, compels us and supernaturally transforms us into His workmanship, a masterpiece, a work-in-progress toward perfection. When a marriage is grounded on the perfect life of Christ, excellence in marriage can be achieved. And this is a goal worth striving for. Is your home and your relationship ever-striving for perfection? Is it grounded on Christ and Christ alone? This is the starting point for marital bliss.

Priority. Secondly, the marriage of Adam and Eve held a place of priority. Genesis 2:24 provides the marriage principle of "leave and cleave." The word *cleave* comes from the Hebrew word *dabag* which means, "to impinge, cling, or adhere to." It's like taking two pieces of wood, bonding them together with wood glue, and then further attaching them with wood screws for good measure. They are so connected together that to separate them would literally destroy both pieces.

This is why God says He hates divorce (Malachi 2:16). He knows that the covenant marriage He ordained with a man and wife is one that so binds them together that separating the two will damage them both greatly. This is why Dale went down to 145 pounds and Jena weighed 97 pounds by the end of the divorce. As we separated in heart, we were destroying ourselves from the inside out. God created the marriage relationship to be a priority. The harsh reality is that many times we make our extended family, our children, our friends, our jobs, and even our church the priority of our lives. God created the marriage between a man and a woman as the first and foremost relational priority in our lives (other than our relationship to Him). When we begin to view our marriages as a priority, we are honoring God's design for marriage since the day He ordained it.

Partnership. Finally, the marriage of Adam and Eve formed a marriage partnership. They were undivided, uniting in spirit, soul, and body. In partnership, you find two people who share in something that includes both the triumphs and the troubles. Genesis 2:24 puts it this way: "they will become one flesh."

From the beginning of time, when God created the heavens and the earth, He declared all was "good." However, upon creating Adam, something was still missing. God said that it was "not good for the man to be alone," for there was no suitable "help-mate" for him (Genesis 2:18). So God created Eve. They were to be partners in life. In partnership, we understand that "what we do, we do together." Whether you have a golf partner, tennis partner, business partner, or Bible study partner, you are working together for one common goal, embracing together both the good and the bad. The same is no less true in marriage.

In fact, it is more critical in marriage than any other relationship in life. Yet many times we find ourselves treating our golf partner, tennis partner, business partner, or Bible study partner better than we do our own spouse. Partnership in marriage means that you and your spouse join hand-in-hand on your specifically ordained journey with God. Any decision you make should be made together with your marriage journey as the focus with the best interest of both of you at heart. All decisions are for the benefit of the marriage partnership, not your own selfish wants and desires.

Ultimately, partnership in marriage includes spending time in prayer, seeking the face of God, and asking Him to lead your marriage (Philippians 4:6). When a marriage is founded on the perfect life of Christ, both husband and wife make each other a priority. They demonstrate genuine partnership and wrap their lives in prayer. That marriage will experience marital bliss by God's design.

Marital Bust

Six months later we again met the couple mentioned in the first paragraph. They were sitting in a newlywed couples Sunday School class with several other couples. When asked how married life was going, the wife quickly responded, "This is not at *all* what I bargained for!" Suddenly, between two weeks and six months, they were no longer experiencing bliss in their marriage. Ever been there? The thoughts of a blissful marriage have been replaced by lost hopes and unfulfilled dreams.

Now let's take a look at Adam and Eve. They have encountered the serpent. Through his craftiness and deceit, there is suddenly no more marital bliss for this couple either. What in the world has happened in this short period of time to these two couples? What has caused the marital bust?

As we continued to study Genesis 2 and 3, we identified three benchmarks of marital bust that were at the heart of our divorce and are instrumental to the breakdown of marriages all over the world today. No one intends to experience marital bust. We surely didn't. And yet it happened. However, if we can identify the destructive forces, we can stand guard for our marriages. Scripture clearly indicates that sin entered the world through the disobedience of Adam and Eve. When sin and disobedience enter a relationship, marital bust is inevitable.

Shame. Sin and disobedience many times turn our homes into places of shame. The sin of Adam and Eve greatly affected their relationship with God and each other. They became so ashamed of their sin that they sewed fig leaves together and covered their nakedness. Nakedness was the only thing they discovered through their newfound wisdom. So many times we make choices only to find out in the end that it was simply a poor decision that didn't turn out at all the way we intended. Adam and Eve wanted to be wise, akin to God. Instead, they felt shame.

When we sin, God through His Holy Spirit brings conviction into our hearts. Conviction says, "My behavior was wrong." Satan, on the other hand, attempts to flood our hearts with shame. Shame says, "There is something wrong with me." It implies that *everybody else is okay, and everybody else is perfect and can do the right things, but I cannot, because there is something wrong with me. I am defective, while everyone else is whole.* When we allow Satan to shame us, we begin to shame others around us to lessen our "singled out" feelings. We begin to shame others with our words to make us feel better about ourselves. This is extremely detrimental to the marriage because it results in two people locked up in tremendous bindings of the enemy. Words such as "you always . . . " and "you never . . . " are at the core of shaming. Shame keeps people so bound in their wrongness that they cannot fulfill the purposes for which God created them. And if shaming isn't making us feel better about ourselves in a situation, we resort to the next tactic: blame.

Blame. The marriage relationship between Adam and Eve developed into a place of blame. They began to blame one another, *and God*, for their own sin. Notice this is the first time we see the age-old strategy of "passing the buck."

Passing the buck started with the first marriage in the Garden of Eden. Today, we practice it to avoid personal responsibility in relationships. Adam blamed Eve, and Adam blamed God. Have you ever blamed God for your situation, when it was your own disobedience that got you there in the first place? Eve blamed the serpent, and we do the same thing. Look at these blaming phrases:

- "Well, I wouldn't have done what I did if you hadn't done what you did!"

- "You made me treat you like that!"
- "I was just reacting to what you said!"

The truth is that we choose each day how we will respond, whether through blaming others or taking responsibility for our own sin. And that is a choice that only we as individuals can make. Nobody can make you do anything. Your behavior is a result of your choice alone. And if ungodly behavior goes unchecked, you can bet you are headed for marital bust.

Pain. If shaming and blaming are common in a marriage, the result is a lot of pain. There were consequences for Adam and Eve's sin that would last a lifetime, and they certainly involved pain. When we sin, we experience the consequences of our actions, and it is usually painful. **One truth about sin is that it will take you farther than you ever intended to go, and keep you longer than you ever intended to stay.** The pain we feel from sin reminds us of our need of Christ. Yet for many, it only makes them cynical and bitter.

If you've ever experienced a cut, then you've experienced pain. After time, a scar forms and you are okay. But if you have ever experienced a cut that continues to be re-opened and never given appropriate time to heal, then you truly understand chronic pain.

During our first marriage and divorce, we used cutting words that went deep, marring the other person. Some of those words left scars that don't hurt as much anymore, but are still reminders of where we've been. Still others left deep wounds on our hearts because they were re-opened time and time again, as the shaming and blaming continued. The recurring inflicting of pain damages the soul. Only the miraculous grace of God could repair the damage.

Once sin entered the garden, with all its blame, shame, and pain, it separated man from God. Adam and Eve suffered great consequences for their sin, but the ultimate consequence was the void left in their hearts when they were separated from their Heavenly Father. And though Adam and Eve desperately desired to be back in close fellowship with God, there was a vast cavern between them that would require a bridge to cross over. God provided that bridge through His Son, Jesus Christ.

Why Am I So Needy?

Just as Adam and Eve were separated from God, we, too, have allowed sin to separate us from God. As we desperately try to find a means to fill this void, we often find ourselves feeling needy. We long to be complete, whole, and in perfect relationship with another. We *are* in need. And though needs are normal, they come with an intense desire that must be satisfied. Many times, we do whatever it takes to have our needs met because we hunger so deeply for their fulfillment.

All of us are aware that we have needs. These needs are legitimate, but we are not always wise in our choice of who or what should meet them. The first year of our marriage, we began to notice how much we needed one another to make us feel complete and whole. Frustration and bitterness grew within our home as we tried so desperately to get the other to fill the insatiable void within our hearts.

I (Jena) came into the marriage with a real need to hear the words "I love you" and "You are so pretty." I didn't understand why, but those words of affirmation were a deep need in my life. I desired to be unconditionally loved, accepted, and trusted. Dale was so young and oblivious to my needs that when I asked him why he never said those things he answered, "When I cease to love you, and when I cease to think you are pretty, I'll let you know." That did nothing except discourage me and drive me further into my quest for fulfillment.

Eve's Curse

Because of sin, Eve was left with a quest to fill her neediness. This quest was formed right out of the curse of her sin, and mothers completely understand her curse! Genesis 3:16 shares with us the curse of pain in childbirth. Many mothers have experienced this pain, so identifying firsthand is not a problem! The last part of the verse, however, is where we either miss it, skip it, or don't really understand it. As we began to study the latter part of the curse, the Spirit gave us understanding and insight that revolutionized our lives and our marriage.

The last part of that verse says, "Your *desire* will be for your husband, and he will rule over you." The word desire comes from the Hebrew word *tshuwqah* (tesh-oo-kaw), which means "a deep longing for," "a craving," "a stretching out after," "of beast to devour." When sin entered the world, Eve no longer knew the safe, secure, and intimate relationship with God. She was left with a void that longed to be filled. Eve now had a natural tendency to crave, stretch, and even devour Adam to get her needs met. When he could not fully do so to her satisfaction, she tried to rule over him. We call this "nagging." As she would demand that her needs be met, incapable Adam would fail to meet those needs, and she became more disappointed and demanding. Yet God declared that Adam would rule over her.

As with Eve, women have a deep longing that needs filling. A woman's greatest need in her life is to develop deep intimacy. She wants to feel safe and secure in her relationships. She wants to know that she is deeply loved and that nothing she does, nothing she is or is not, will change that love. She also wants to be confident in the commitment of the one with whom she has a relationship. She wants to know that no matter what happens, her husband is committed. While the need for deep intimacy and security is not exclusive to women, it is the primary need of most women.

In modern culture, when a woman begins to make demands, she is considered a nag. In reality she is behaving within the curse of Eve, with her unquenchable longing and stretching out for intimacy. The truth is, there is no earthly relationship that can fully meet that need.

God hand-carved the void in your life so you would see your need for Him. Then He sent Jesus to completely fill the void. If someone or something else could fill that void, then Jesus' death as our Savior would have been in vain. And when we look to other things to fulfill us, we make a mockery of Jesus Christ and His death on the cross. We also elevate someone else to a position that belongs to Jesus, and this is idolatry. Christ will share His glory with no one.

Jesus Christ is the only one who can fully meet your need. And yet, spouses, that does not get you off the hook. For every curse there is a calling. Men, now that you know your wife's deepest need for intimacy, safety, and security, you possess the wonderful privilege of pointing her to the very One who can so fulfill that need. By doing so, you enhance freedom in the life of your wife. You free her from demanding what she needs from you or others. You free her from being disappointed when nothing else satisfies. You also free yourself from living a defeated lifestyle. All those times when you did your very best to meet your wife's needs and it was never good enough are past. You never have to feel like a failure again. What an awesome calling for men to lead their wives to the unconditional love of Jesus Christ.

Women, it is so incredible that Christ's love never changes, no matter what. Romans 8:38–39 says this: "For I am convinced that neither death nor life, neither angels nor demons, neither the present nor the future, nor any powers, neither height nor depth, nor anything else in all creation, will be able to separate us from the love of God that is in Christ Jesus, our Lord." Through His Son, He wants to fill the void that sin left. His commitment proved true, all the way to the cross. He can be trusted. His love is so unconditional that nothing you do or don't do will change His love for you. He loves the very best of you and the very worst. He loves you, warts and all. And He wants to fill you with His love to overflowing, so that His love will pour off of you onto a world that so desperately needs to see and feel it. How it must break the heart of God to offer His only beloved Son to meet our deepest needs, and watch us shun this incredible gift while searching for what we think is better!

Will you allow God to fill every crevice of your heart with His love and commitment to you? This decision will totally and radically change your life and marriage.

Adam's Curse

Adam was also cursed for his sin. His curse involved the sweating and toiling of work (Genesis 3: 17–19). And with that curse came a root need that is evident in every man.

Meet Jake. Jake had worked for months building a deck for his home. He wasn't just building the deck because he was dying to do so. He was building this deck for his family to enjoy. We have heard countless men make this statement: "Everything I do, I do for my family; sometimes, I feel it's never good enough!" Jake had visions of late afternoon cookouts with friends and family. From this deck, he would be able to watch his children play in the yard. And he could sit in the morning shade, drinking coffee and visiting with his wife. No, this wasn't just a deck. It was a monument of Jake's dedication to his family and his internal sense of accomplishment.

The day of unveiling was finally here. Jake had finished his deck right on schedule for a Labor Day cookout. They invited friends and family and put food on the grill. It was going to be a wonderful day. As everyone started to arrive, Jake proudly escorted them to the deck. The compliments were overwhelming, yet something was missing. As the others raved about the new deck, Jake realized his wife remained silent. It was as if she didn't even care.

At the end of the day, Jake sat down to share his hurt feelings with his wife, Tammy. With tears in his eyes, Jake looked at Tammy and said, "Everyone was happy for me, and made me feel special . . . everyone but you. You could care less about what I do for you or this family! Does anything I do for you really matter?"

The depth of this statement, when it is fully understood by couples, will cause them to take a long hard look at how they treat each other. As good as the compliments were from all of Jake's friends and family, he most wanted to hear praise from Tammy. Of all the people Jake wanted to impress, Tammy was on top of the list. When that did not happen, Jake was deeply hurt and felt insignificant. What he did didn't seem to matter to Tammy at all.

If you have ever spent much time in an airport, you have heard all kinds of conversations as people wait for their plane to arrive. Men's conversations seem to focus around one main element: what they do. The fact is that most men define who they are by what they do. It provides for them a sense of importance and validation.

A man's greatest need is to be important. He wants to feel that he makes a difference and that what he does matters. He wants to be appreciated and valued. Though many have a tough outward appearance, the truth is that they still have a deep need to feel they have a purpose to accomplish in life. And when they accomplish it, they need to be recognized for it. Though the need to feel important and valued is primarily seen in men, many women share this need as well.

This is precisely what resulted for Adam. He lost his position of importance as king of Eden, and now had a deep longing to get it back. He wanted to feel that importance in position once again. If you have ever been frustrated at your attempts to succeed in something and failed, then you can readily identify with the pain of feeling unimportant. In the arena of marriage, feelings of insignificance can lead to marital bust. A wife seeks to have her needs met by her husband. When this does not occur, she not only gets discouraged and demanding, but her husband feels defeated. Why? Because in his futile attempts to meet her needs and thus feel important, he fails.

Yet he was never created with the capacity to fully meet her needs, and therefore, as he tries and fails, he becomes more defeated. Typically, after a period of failures, he will quit trying altogether and shut down emotionally in the relationship. No man with the innate need to feel valued and important will put himself continually in positions to fail. As with women's need for intimacy, no earthly relationship can fully meet a man's need for importance.

A Word for Men

Men, God left the void in your life so that you would let Him fill that need with Himself. He can strengthen you in the deepest recesses of your heart. Unfortunately, you think you know of other things that will fill you, so you stuff your hearts with all the wrong things. If you can accomplish enough in the work world, have enough money, live in bigger houses, drive nicer cars, own a boat, be the best on the golf course, at the hunting lodge, have the most trophies, and even get into another relationship, *some how, some way these things will make me important.* When you realize that these things fail to fill the void, then you will run to Jesus. Jesus Christ is the only one who can satisfy the deep longing in your soul to find importance, value and worth. You are important simply because He created you with a specific purpose in mind. Jeremiah 29:11 says, "'For I know the plans I have for you,' declares the LORD, 'plans to prosper you and not to harm you, plans to give hope and a future.'"

Isn't it awesome to know that your very existence was for the pleasurable will of God? From the very moment of your creation, He had plans for you. And His plans are for your good. There is not a single bird that falls to the ground that our Father does not know about. And how much more important are you to Him than a bird (Luke 12:24)?

The summer before Jena's senior year in high school, she had a horrible automobile accident. Because of her injuries, she was rushed straight to the emergency room for immediate attention. Her mother and father rushed to the hospital as soon as they heard the news. As her mother made it to the room, she stood over Jena's bed and made this simple but life-changing statement, "God left you on this earth for a purpose. You'd best find out what it is and do it with all of your heart." God has a plan for your life. You are an important part of His plan. He has left you on this earth for a purpose. You'd best find out what it is and do it with all of your heart.

A Word for Women

Now women, don't think that this gets you off of the hook either! With this curse on the men comes a calling for you as well. You have the wonderful privilege of pointing your husband to the One who made Him important in the first place. It is imperative that your husband knows that you appreciate what he does for you and your family, but more importantly that God sees great value in him. Don't miss the opportunity to be grateful by verbally recognizing your husband's hard work and sacrifice for you. And point him to the very One who can give Him spiritual value and direction for your family now and in the future.

It is so incredible to know that you were created with a great purpose. Just think; God has wonderful plans for our lives that are one, obedient, submissive step away. Yet many times we are too stubborn and self-reliant to follow Him. Will you commit yourself to seek God's intimate and important purpose for your life? Will you let Him fill that void? Make yourself available for His plans and you will begin an incredible journey with your Savior.

Vicious Cycle

We have come to recognize our needs for intimacy and importance as individuals and discovered how Christ is the only one who can meet those needs. When we seek other ways to meet our needs, we get caught in a vicious cycle that too many times spins out of control.

In our marriage this cycle was spinning faster than you can imagine. Jena had a tremendous need to be needed and loved. When I (Dale) did not fully meet that need, she went to church and taught a Bible study. After all, the women at church loved her and needed her to encourage and help them. Jena began to spend so much time with the women of her Bible study that I began to feel that I was moving down Jena's totem pole of priority and importance. So I headed to the golf course. There I could compete, accomplish something by attempting to win all the matches, and thus feel good about myself. Jena saw that I was spending more time at the golf course than with her, so she began to feel that I didn't love her and was not committed to her. She began pouring her life into singing and writing musicals . . . busy, busy, busy. I assumed that I was not important to her anymore, so I headed to the office to climb the corporate ladder. After all, the people there acknowledged my efforts and affirmed me for a job well done. And the cycle went on and on. Jena even recalls the thoughts at the birth of our first child, Cole, being, "Well, maybe when Dale sees the pain I go through to give him a son, he will love me more."

Do you hear and see the neediness and the desperate measures we took to fulfill our needs? This vicious cycle of neediness is going on in households all over the world today, creating marital bust in dynamic proportions. With no concern for the other person's feelings, we continue in an effort to take care of ourselves. If somebody was hurt in the process, who cares? It's all about me.

We learned through our divorce that all we had was Jesus, and He was all we needed. His love, His goodness,

His presence is the only thing that can fill the deep crevices of our lives and make us healthy and whole. When we learned that, we were able to minister to one another, pointing each other to the "need meet-er."

Freedom: Stopping the Cycle

As a child, we would have definitely said that the icing was the best part of the cake. As adults, however, the best part has become the cake and not the icing. Icing just happens to be a little sweet extra that comes along with the cake.

As we allow Christ to fill the neediness in our lives, we no longer stretch out, starving for love, affirmation, intimacy, and importance, to our spouse. When Christ begins to fill those areas in our lives, He becomes the foundation, or the "cake," of our hearts. The encouragement, affirmation, love, and acceptance from our mate is wonderful and welcomed, but it is not what we stake our lives on. It becomes a nice addition to the fullness we already experience in and through Christ. Soon, your favorite part becomes the cake, and the icing you receive from your mate is just the sweet, added extra.

Galatians 5:1 says, "It is for freedom that Christ has set us free." Christ came to set you free from sin and from death, not so that you could be enslaved to the neediness of one another. Christ set you free so that you could be free to minister His love to one another, because your need has already been fulfilled.

You can be free from the **demands** of your mate's neediness, because Christ meets their needs. You just offer extra encouragement. You can be free from **disappointment** when your mate is not meeting your needs, because you no longer expect them to be the primary person who meets your needs. They are the "icing on the cake." And finally, you are free from feelings of **defeat** that come when your mate doesn't meet your expectations. When both you and your spouse are daily filling yourselves with Christ, you can each be free to love, encourage, and affirm your spouse out of **devotion**, not out of duty. Doesn't that sound like freedom to you?

There is so much freedom in understanding how deeply the Father loves and cares for us. Our only requirement is to walk with Him, allowing Him to fill us to overflowing with His love. Then we are free to minister to our mates. Why? "So that Christ may dwell in your hearts through faith. And I pray that you, being rooted and established in love, may have power, together with all the saints, to grasp how wide and long and high and deep is the love of Christ" (Ephesians 3:17–18). The cake is there. All we have to do is feast on it.

Shame, blame, and **pain** took us down a road toward marital bust that we never dreamed we would travel. Friend, if you have found that your marriage is not what you bargained for, see if the characteristics of marital bust have found a place to lodge in your home. Ask your heavenly Father to tear down those areas that have crept into your life. Then your relationship can be above and beyond what you could have ever imagined. That is God's desire for our homes.

Philippians 1:6 says, "being confident of this, that he who began a good work in you will carry it on to completion until the day of Christ Jesus." Let God do His continuing work in your life and the life of your spouse. Ground your marriage in the elements of marital bliss, founded on the perfect life of Christ. You can be confident in His working as you allow Him to refine you.

Chapter Four

A Look at our Legacy

A s we continued the process of identifying how the two of us contributed to the breakdown of our marriage, we realized that someone else played a major role in destroying our union. That someone was the enemy, Satan. Whether you believe it or not, you have an enemy who is against you and your marriage. His goal is utter ruin for you and your home, and he will stop at nothing until he reaches that goal. Yet our confidence is that we are overcomers through Jesus Christ, our Lord!

The Enemy

If you have ever read John 10:10, you understand that God's Word tells us that the thief, Satan, comes to steal, kill, and destroy. Have you ever thought about what exactly it is that the enemy, Satan, is trying to kill, steal, and destroy? Scripture tells us that God holds us in the palm of

His righteous right hand. Nothing can pluck us out of it. So what then can Satan steal, kill, or destroy?

The answer is found in the last part of the verse. The enemy is trying to kill, steal, and destroy anything that would give you the abundant life Christ offers. Make no mistake about it. If you are a child of the King, you have an enemy, and he will do whatever he can to make you ineffective in the Kingdom, since he can no longer have you for his own.

As we studied our individual needs, we began to see that Satan attacked our minds. He has deceived us into thinking that other things can fill the voids in our lives— the holes only Christ can fill. God's Word tells us that Satan truly is a liar. John 8:44 says this: "You belong to your father, the devil, and you want to carry out your father's desire. He was a murderer from the beginning, not holding to the truth, for there is no truth in him. When he lies, he speaks his native language, for he is a liar and the father of lies."

Lies are the way of the enemy. He lies to us about who we are and who God is. He is like a scheming snake, seeking ways to divide and destroy us. We are told in Ephesians 6.11, "Put on the full armor of God so that you can take your stand against the devil's schemes." So while Satan does not deserve our focus and attention, we shouldn't underestimate or ignore his plots against the children of God.

The Enemy's Strategy

We believe that the enemy's strategy works something like this: we enter the world with needs. The enemy deceives us into thinking that other people or things will meet those needs. We exchange the truth of what will meet our needs (Christ) for the enemy's lie. Proverbs 23:7 says, "As he thinks in his heart, so is he" (NKJV). We begin to behave in ways that reflect our belief in the lie. Before we know it, Satan has a stronghold in our lives. We are slaves to the never-ending quest to fill our neediness. We are no longer free to enjoy the abundant life God has planned for us. The diagram below depicts the path the enemy uses.

Needs ➤ Deception ➤ Lie ➤ Behavior ➤ Stronghold

Maybe the lie you have accepted as truth is, "If I could just make a little more money, then I would feel important and valuable around here." Or maybe it is, "If I could just look like that movie star or model, then I would be loved and accepted." These, friend, are lies. They are lies that can so consume you and your behavior that they become your focus, and you lose sight of God in the process. That is the enemy's desire: for you to lose sight of your Heavenly Father altogether.

In this chapter, we will study how family upbringing can affect a marriage. We pray that the Spirit of God will reveal some lies that may have been passed down to you from previous generations. This is not a parent-bashing chapter, nor is it intended to degrade your family heritage in any form. God's Word plainly tells us to honor our parents that our days may be long (Exodus 20:12), and this is a command that we must follow. You may have wonderful attributes in your family, which leave beautiful legacies to pass from generation to generation. Yet there may also be some characteristics that are not so admirable. You may need to remove them from your family line and replace them with the characteristics of Christ.

Isn't it an incredible thought that God could use you to defeat some lies that have been passed from generation to generation, holding your family captive? This is why Christ came, to set the captives free.

If you are held captive to the lies of the enemy and feel downtrodden by his deceit, be of good cheer. Your Father has sent His Son to set you free. And he who the Son sets free is free indeed (John 8:36). You know what *indeed* means? *Indeed* means "really, for certain." When the Son sets you free from the enemy's lies, you are really, really free, for sure.

Getting to the Root

In our quest for freedom, the Lord began to show us, as a couple and as individuals, how He had been working and teaching us long ago. We also learned how we missed His teachings. He began bringing memories back up from our pasts to give us a second chance at this thing Proverbs calls "wisdom and understanding." He reminded Jena of a time when she was growing up. Her grandparents, Nannie and James Mathis, lived on a farm in Pavo, Georgia. She loved to go to their house and see all of the fruits and vegetables that were reaped from the seeds sown months before. As she reflected on this memory, Jena recalled learning about how an apple can reflect Satan's attack on our lives.

When a flower buds forth on an apple tree, an apple will soon be formed. Many times, however, a worm attaches itself to the flower bud. Then the fruit of the apple grows around the bud or seedling. So when you see a hole in an apple, it is not that the worm has worked its way in, but it has worked its way out! This is what has happened to many of us. As children, the enemy, like a worm, has attached a lie to the seedling or bud of our hearts. The fruit, or behavior, of our lives has grown around that lie.

So often, we try various methods to fix or clean up the fruit of our lives. Maybe we work on communication, or our problems with anger, depression, eating disorders, performance, perfectionism. The list could go on and on. While it's admirable to work on these things, we cannot be so consumed by them that we do not deal with the root of the problem(s). Many of these behaviors are mere "fruit" that stem from a "worm" attached to the root in our life, as well as, the roots in our family's life. Romans 11:16 says, "If the part of the dough offered as firstfruits is holy, then the whole batch is holy; if the root is holy, so are the branches." Our goal is for you to deal with the root lies so that the root of your heart will become whole and holy as you walk in Truth. Then the "fruit" of your life and marriage will be holy as you become a reflection of Christ.

To start this journey, we began asking the Holy Spirit to reveal to us the lies that we had never been able to see. We couldn't see them because they had become such a regular pattern of behavior. We desperately wanted to get rid of the lies that were eating at the root of our hearts, and replace them with truth. Then we could have a good root that would produce good fruit. You might be able to identify with our discoveries.

Jena's Lie—The 99 Syndrome

I (Jena) grew up in a loving home with wonderful Christian parents who taught me the value of church, servanthood, and commitment. I was confident that God would provide, because my father and mother worked very hard and sacrificed to provide for me. There was one thing, though, that I was not so confident in—myself. From an early age, I felt that I was not good enough. I can remember times in my life when I made a 99 on a math test and felt that I should have made 100. Feeling that my parents would be disappointed in my lack of perfection, I struggled to be the best, but the feeling stayed the same. I was just a 99 . . . not quite good enough.

When I was a small child, the enemy began to fuel these thoughts. He fed my thought life with continual belittling and condemnation about my less-than-acceptable and less-than-perfect life. These feelings eventually caused me to question God and His love for me. I bought into the lie that I wasn't good enough, and my behavior reflected it. I can remember playing on the playground with my best friend, and another girl coming along and taking my friend away. The enemy taunted me in my thinking: "You're just not good enough. If you were, your friend would have stayed with you!" I remember the one beauty pageant I entered—I was awarded 1st runner up. The attacks of the enemy ran through my mind as the deceptive voice of Satan cried out, "Jena, you're not quite good enough. If you were, you would have won this pageant." I remember striving so hard to graduate #1 in my class and being #9. Again I was not quite good enough.

I not only believed the lie, but I began looking for affirmations of the lie in my life. Soon it became a stronghold for Satan—the stronghold of performance. I so wanted the approval of others and of God that I did whatever anybody wanted me to do and tried desperately to be the best. If I was the best at everything I did, I felt I could somehow win their approval and love (my primary need). I thought that love from others and God was strictly conditional upon my actions. And though I worked hard and gained the approval of some, I was miserable on the inside, exhausted from the struggle of people-pleasing performance. This stronghold of the 99 syndrome held me captive, even though Christ wanted me free.

Dale's Lie—The Competitor's Syndrome

I (Dale) also grew up in a Christian home, where I was taught the value of church, hard work, and fairness. I was born the younger of twin boys, and thus learned quickly the importance of competing to be number one. I had to fight for my own identity. I did not want to be Dave's twin; I wanted Dave to be known as Dale's twin. So I competed in baseball, football, golf, girls, grades, and popularity. As I continued my competition quest, the enemy took advantage of this opportunity to lie to me. After all, my number one need to feel important would be validated when I competed and succeeded above all others.

I bought into the lie that I had to be the best at everything, or at least be better than my brother, in order to be valuable and important. Everything I did either supported or confirmed the lie. This carried over into my view of God. I thought that I had to compete for God's love—to be perfect and successful in order to be loved and accepted by Him. I was caught in a stronghold of self-sufficiency that Jena and I call the Competitor's Syndrome.

Can you identify with one of these lies? Or perhaps you have another lie that you have accepted as truth from the father of lies. Maybe you grew up believing that the only way to be accepted and loved was by looking pretty, and you have found yourself trapped by anorexia or bulimia. Maybe you are caught in an addiction to food, alcohol, or another substance. Or perhaps you learned at an early age that possessions bring happiness. Today you are totally dependent on what you own. Even now, we pray for God to show you the lies, so that you can uproot them and re-plant the truth in your life.

Climbing the Family Tree

Not only do lies from the enemy cause us to have an unhealthy view of ourselves and God, but our family histories, both good and bad, have a profound effect on how we relate to others. Studying our families of origin allows us to identify the struggles and stresses that occur in marriage because of family dynamics.

When we began this process of healing our marriage, we began by taking pencils and drawing out our family trees, starting with our grandparents and moving down to ourselves. (Note: If you choose to do this as well, please keep in mind that we are mainly looking for those people who most influenced your life and upbringing. Should you have been raised in a foster home, or by your grandparents, simply record those who most influenced your life.)

We then began to write down the characteristics of each person on the tree. One-word descriptions, communication patterns, responses to conflict or stresses, and repeated patterns of behavior were just a few things we recorded. Suddenly, we began to see how many of these habits, coping mechanisms, and attitudes had been passed down to us. Some of these qualities and characteristics were causing some differences and conflicts between us. Not that either person's upbringing was better, right, or wrong—they were just different. The enemy loves to enhance our differences and drive a wedge within our relationship.

Jena's Tree

My paternal grandparents were very work-oriented and carried high levels of commitment to both church and family. They taught my father the value of knowing and loving God's Word and being very active and committed to the church. My grandfather loved Coke and peanuts, and always had some for our family when we came to visit. He loved a good laugh. My father then grew into a hard worker with strong commitments, who was funny and a wonderful provider.

My maternal grandparents were also very hard workers and were very service-oriented. They were very friendly and liked to be around people. They lived on a farm and helped many people who were in need around their community. Both of my maternal grandparents died during our divorce, which brought me face-to-face with the certainty of death and the brevity of life. At their funerals, people

I did not know came to me, sharing what my grandparents had done for them. My grandparents had received no accolades, no applause; they just did good to those around them because they loved as Christ loves. Because of their example, my mother was a very loving, fun, affectionate, giving person. What a sobering thought to think that children become what they see day in and day out.

When my parents had conflict, they talked it out until it was resolved. Their motto was, "Don't let the sun go down on your wrath." So they worked hard at a resolution, even if it took all night. They also spent the majority of their time together. So I came into our marriage believing that I was a 99 (not quite good enough), confident that I would always be provided for, and willing to give and serve when I saw a need. I also shared my parents' value of laughter and loving God's Word. Finally, I thought that everything should be talked out, and that Dale and I should spend all of our time together. After all, that is what happened in my home, and everybody's home looked the same, right?

Dale's Tree

My paternal grandparents were all about ministry. My grandfather was a Baptist preacher, committed to ministering to others. Many people have told me how he spoke the Word of God boldly and unashamedly. Today I share his heartbeat to preach and teach the Word in ministry to others.

My father was the oldest of five children and so he felt responsible for leadership and keeping peace in the home in his father's absence. My father was the ultimate peacemaker, a trait he learned from his family environment.

My maternal grandparents were some of the hardest-working people in America. They married during the height of the Depression and learned the value of hard work and partnership. They were very service-oriented and giving. I can tell many stories about the joys of playing in my grandmother's backyard, of her having candy waiting for me when I got off the school bus. The attention she gave me made me feel like I was the most important person in the world. My mother thus became a hard-working and giving person, just like her parents. She showed her love through service to her children, just as my grandmother had done.

My parents brought their histories with them into their marriage. I never saw conflict in my home because my father was the peacemaker. His family motto was "Tomorrow will be a better day." My parents worked incredibly hard during the week, so they spent the weekends doing things they enjoyed, like playing golf and serving the family. Many times, they simply did their own thing.

So I came into the marriage believing that to be important, I had to be number one in Jena's life (Competitor's Syndrome.) I competed for Jena's attention, and when conflict arose, I went to bed, thinking, *Tomorrow will be a better day*. I also expected to do my own thing when the weekend arrived.

Can you see how differently we were raised? When we realized these differences we gained a completely different perspective of our marriage. Jena came in with a need for affirming words that told her "You are a 100," "You are beautiful," "I love you." She expected to talk through our conflict and spend most of our time together. I came into the marriage with a need to feel valued and important. I also desired physical affection from Jena. I did whatever it took to keep the peace, and wanted time away to do my own thing. Are you beginning to see why we had struggles in our marriage?

Joined Together

Our first year of marriage, like so many, was difficult, as we tried desperately to get the other to meet our needs. When conflict arose, Jena wanted to talk it out, and I wanted to go to bed in hopes that "tomorrow would be a better day." When I went to bed, that confirmed to Jena that she must be a 99, because if I really loved her I would stay up and talk it out. The sad thing is that I had no idea what I was communicating through my actions—that I was damaging the relationship. I just thought I had to work hard, provide for my family, and keep the peace.

At one point that first year, we had a major disagreement. As the fight escalated, I (Dale) chose to go to bed. This was one of the ways I sought to keep peace (at least then we weren't fighting). Jena got frustrated and left the house. She drove all over town until 2 A.M. When she finally returned home, I was fast asleep. For the little girl who thought she was a 99, I just affirmed the lie as truth. What does someone struggling with the 99 Syndrome want their spouse to do? Jena wanted me to summon the police, call her mother and father, wake up the pastor, send out the bloodhounds, do whatever it took to find her. Why? *Because she was worth it.* Jena desired, even longed for confirmation that she is a 100-plus in my life. She, like so many wives, wanted me to demonstrate that I valued her as my bride and gift from God. When that did not occur, the pain was intense, the lie confirmed, and the stronghold continued.

Do you see what happened? It was not that Jena's ways were right and mine wrong or Jena's ways wrong and mine right. They were simply different. And neither of us acknowledged the differences. Our very ignorance of our family dynamics caused deeply injured feelings, captivity to the lies of the enemy, and strongholds of behaviors. Our marriage was not free, it was in bondage. We were slaves to our own neediness and lack of understanding.

We are all familiar with cause and effect. We teach our children about actions and consequences every day. If you tell your child not to touch the hot stove and they touch it, they will get burned. From that day forward, that child remembers that if he touches the hot stove, he will get burned. Just as cause and effect teaches a child about a hot stove, we also learn by cause and effect in our relationship to others. Our backdrop of experience, our family dynamics, the good and the not-so-good things we have witnessed have a huge impact on our relationships. We pray that the Holy Spirit is turning on some lights for you to see some truth that might have been hidden from view.

In Your Marriage

Has the enemy been holding your marriage captive to the lies he has fed you and in the blinders he has placed over your eyes? When the Holy Spirit begins to shine His Light into our lives, we are set free from the dark hidden areas and the deceptive lies of the enemy. John 1:4–5 says, "In him was life, and that life was the light of men. The light shines in the darkness, but the darkness has not understood it." The darkness cannot overcome the light. Through Christ we see a life that was a light for us to live by. Do you know where freedom from the enemy comes from? It comes from following in the light of Christ.

For some, digging deep into the recesses of your hearts and homes may be easy. For others, it may be the toughest and most painful experience you've ever had. Facing a difficult and painful past is never easy. Our fleshly nature desires to leave it there, push it back down when it attempts to resurface, or pretend it never happened. Yet to truly be set free, we must remove the bad roots that are bearing bad fruit in our marriage. Can this happen? Is it even possible? We want to encourage you by sharing what God did to release us from the enemy's snare. However, there was one requirement, and that was to cooperate with Him through obedience. Dear friend, God can only completely use what has been completely broken, and He desires to use you to display His glory.

His Word promises that He gives you everything that you need to have life and godliness through knowing the truth about Him (2 Peter 1:3). He also promises to be the restorer of those things that your enemy has sought to destroy. He takes all things and works them together for good (Romans 8:28).

Tearing Down the Strongholds

As we discovered the lies and sought to destroy them, God took us on a path toward healing and wholeness, in close communion with Him. He showed us that we must first **acknowledge** the lies that have held us captive. Just as an alcoholic must admit that there is a problem, we have to admit the lies that we have accepted as truth. The Bible urges us to put on the whole armor of God (Ephesians 6:11), and the first piece of armor is the belt of truth. If we want to render the enemy powerless, we must admit the lies so that they can be replaced with the truth.

We then began to **appeal** to God in prayer. So many of us take for granted the privilege and the power of prayer. God longs for us to call out to Him. And He doesn't need some glorified, embellished prayer. He just wants your heart, in desperate need of His saving grace and truth.

When we were going through our divorce, I (Jena) can remember climbing into the red bunk bed night after night with our son, Cole, and crying myself to sleep. Many nights, prayers went before the Lord from a wounded heart, and they were as simple as "Help me." No doubt these simple, short prayers were the most precious prayers ever prayed; for they were prayed from a heart that had come to the end of itself and had come begging the Father to help. I (Dale) remember night after night, as I approached the house that used to be a home, praying "God go before me, I don't think I can do this anymore." In the helpless, hopeless moments, we must appeal to our Heavenly Father. He longs to hear from us.

Philippians 4:6–7 says this, "Do not be anxious about anything, but in everything, by prayer and petition, with thanksgiving, present your requests to God. And the peace of God, which transcends all understanding, will guard your hearts and your minds in Christ Jesus." After acknowledging our strongholds and appealing to God in prayer, it was time for us to **adopt** a new way of thinking— to obey His Word.

Picture a tape recorder in your brain, playing lies over and over again until you've accepted them as truth. This is exactly what happened to us. Jena continually heard,

"You're a 99 and will always be a 99." Jena expected things to turn out certain ways because of her false belief system. And the tape continued to play. My lie played continuously in my mind as well, saying, "I will win at whatever cost." We had to stop the tape, take it out, and replace it with the truth. This was a process. We had lived the lie for many years, and we had to intentionally strive to practice believing and walking in our newfound truth, the truth God had for us.

Jena, you're not a 99, you are a 100 plus. Not because of anything good in you, but because My Son lives in your life.

Dale, you don't have to be perfect, you don't have to win to be important. You are important, because I sent My Son to die for you. You are important to Me and My Kingdom.

It's time for truth to become your new way of thinking and living.

We had no idea how to begin this quest for truth, so we decided to get up every morning and simply ask God this question: "What do You think about me? Would You guide me into all truth?" God walked us through the pages of His Word and daily showed us just what He thought of us.

- God showed us that we were created in His image and for His glory (Genesis 1:26).

- God cares deeply for us, holding every tear we've shed in a bottle (Psalm 56:8).
- We are 100s because He lives within us (Jeremiah 29:11).
- We can do all things through Christ who gives us strength (Philippians 4:13).
- With God, nothing is impossible (Matthew 19:26).
- He has called us by name. We are His. He is with us. And He loves us (Isaiah 43:1–5).

The words of our Father, Savior, and Friend continued to pour over us like fresh water to quench our sick and thirsty souls. His Word began to sweep over us and change our outlook and behavior, freeing us from the lies that had held us. We found the truth and that truth set us free (John 8:32). The truth of Christ destroyed the enemy's hold over us. We were no longer in bondage to the lie that affected our marriage, preventing us from ministering to a lost and dying world. Our adversary was defeated! The blood of Jesus Christ and the word of our testimony defeated him (Revelation 12:11).

There comes a day of reckoning. There comes a day when you can no longer blame your past or the failures of others (especially your immediate family and friends). There comes a day when you must take a step toward freedom's path, acknowledging your stronghold, appealing to God in prayer, adopting a new way of thinking, and living in the freedom Christ offers you. Friend, there is victory in Jesus! Don't let the enemy have a hold over you anymore.

You can be free in Jesus Christ. Free from the lies, free from the pain of past sin, free from your past struggles, free from your differences, and free to glorify Him through your life and marriage. Hallelujah, what a Savior!

Chapter Five

The Shame Train

uring our journey toward reconciliation, God opened our eyes to see many things we had not seen before. We were amazed at what the Holy Spirit was revealing to us about ourselves, our upbringing, our needs, our motives, and our hearts. Some of it was good, but some of it was despicable. As we began to see the sin that was penetrating our hearts and lives, God gave us a new perspective of ourselves.

Like uneaten leftovers in our refrigerator, we often allow sin to take up residence in our hearts until it rots. When we allow the enemy to deceive us with his slant on the sin in our lives, he distorts our way of thinking by flooding our minds with shame.

Shame is a real emotion. It is a feeling that everybody else is normal and okay, but you are not. It's not just that you made mistakes, did something wrong. Shame says there is something wrong with *you*—with who you are. You are defective, either physically, mentally, or emotionally, while everybody else has it all together.

There is a huge difference between *conviction* over sin and *shame* from our sin. Conviction says, "My behavior was wrong, but I am still a normal person. I made a mistake and need to confess and repent and move forward with God." Shame says, "I am a mistake. I am abnormal. I mess up all the time and I just can't get it together. Everybody else can get it right, but not me. There is something wrong with me. God must be disgusted at what He made in me." Shame leaves people very defeated with no hope, but conviction can draw you to your Savior and take you even deeper in relationship with Him. Conviction leads to freedom and refreshment (Acts 3:19). Yet many of us are still rotting in the devil's snare of shame.

Have you ever thought, "If others really knew me they would not like me. If they really knew the sin that has been or is currently in my life, they would hate me." If you have ever thought this, then you are carrying shame in your life. The enemy is using it as a means to keep you captive.

Many may carry shame from sin that was self-inflicted. You sinned on your own accord, out of your own choosing. Still others may be carrying around shame from a sin that someone else inflicted upon them. They were sinned against. Regardless, shame can take root in your heart, leaving you stagnant in your relationships.

As a child, I (Jena) had extremely yellow teeth because of a medicine I had to take. Many people began to call me "Greena"—a nickname that embarrassed me. For them it was all in jest, but for a child who was just beginning to find her place as a young lady, this was a shaming experience. It was so shaming that I was extremely self-conscious about my teeth. I didn't show my teeth much, even when I spoke or smiled.

Along with the shame I already felt came my own willful disobedience to God, which carried consequences into adulthood. During our divorce trial, Dale and I accused, questioned, and blamed each other in an effort to obtain custody of our children. We accused each other of affairs, child neglect, child abuse, and mental instability. We hurled words that cut to the core. The devastation and pain were indescribable. It was as if we were dreaming, hoping we hadn't really said those things. But it was no dream, and the wounds inflicted were deep.

The enemy added these hurtful words to my past. He planted a seed of shame deep into my heart which took root and left me too wounded to minister to others. I felt that I was no good, ruined for life. Many times, feelings like these lead us down a road that God never intended for us to travel. In our ministry, Dale and I call it the "Shame Train."

The Shame Train looks something like this:

Hurt
Anger
Bitterness
Shame
Performance   Destruction

When we disobey God or when someone sins against us, our heart is hurt. If we do not deal with that hurt, but suppress it or ignore it in hopes that it will go away, we soon become angry. Sometimes we don't even recognize the source of our anger. We find ourselves angry for allowing sin into our lives. We find ourselves angry with others who might have prevented shameful experiences. Sometimes, we are angry with God for allowing our sinfulness or the sinfulness of others. This soon leads us to bitterness—a ceaseless, continual focus on the hurt that leaves a constant bad taste in our mouths. Before we are even aware of it, we have become immensely depressed. We are staying in bed longer, dwelling on the hurt. We begin having warped thoughts as the enemy continues his deception and lies. Suddenly our behavior begins to reflect one of two extremes. We either begin to perform our way into feeling good about ourselves again, or we begin to self-destruct through anger, control and manipulation because there is no hope for restoration.

I (Jena) chose the road of performance. After all, I had already bought into the enemy's original lie that I was just a 99 and never measured up. Moving from shame to performance as an escape wasn't a big leap. I hoped to perform my way into the hearts of others and God by my new personality, intelligence, and appearance. But my hopes for happiness soon deteriorated as the condemning feelings still consumed my thinking. I wasn't sure who I was anymore because the old Jena had become lost in the new-found Jena. The voice inside me kept saying, "Because of all the sin in my life, I have no value whatsoever." Soon I was convinced God would always be disappointed in me. The enemy thought he had won.

Dale, like many men, moved toward destruction. When feelings of shame and hurt cut him to the core, he came out fighting. His battle method was, "I will destroy whomever or whatever is not on my side." His mentality: "If I can somehow win and come out on top at the end of the day—be the one still standing—then I will be important and a success." Dale marched to the drumbeat of "If you're not for me, then you're against me."

The destruction in his life showed up as a driving need to be in control, to have all the answers, and be in charge. Because of hurt and anger, which led to bitterness, Dale allowed the enemy to fuel the destruction with lies and deceit. Depression set in as he realized that he was not in control and didn't have all the answers. Believing that his importance came from his abilities and not from God, Dale became void of emotion. Consequently, he continued on this path of self-destruction. His plan, to destroy whomever or whatever got in his way, ended up destroying him in the process. There was no victory in that at all.

Understanding Our Shame

The word *shame* appears in various forms throughout Scripture, its Greek and Hebrew carrying similar definitions. However, one defining word that continually appeared within the definitions was *confusion*. As we began to study and ask for the Holy Spirit's guidance towards truth and understanding, God allowed us to understand this reality: as we travel farther on the shame train, we forget who God created us to be. We become *confused* about who we really are because we're so consumed by the shame we feel before God and others.

And who do we know is the author of confusion? The enemy himself. Satan holds us captive in our shame by confusing us about who we are. He causes us to question ourselves and God. And what did the enemy use to cause Adam and Eve to stumble into their sin? He caused them to question God's command. He began to enslave them through doubt and confusion. And in the end, they were ashamed. The enemy still uses the same old strategy today, shaming believers into captivity.

Consider a woman who grew up in a home with sexual abuse or was raped earlier in her life. Sometimes the intense hurt that mars her heart puts her on the shame train, and she doesn't even know it. She continually struggles with her weight and cannot understand why. Then she realizes that her addiction to food is a response to her immense shame. In order to protect herself from further physical abuse, she becomes overweight. *If I am unattractive to men, they won't hurt me.* The shame train brings her to self-destruction and confusion.

Or think about a wife who finds that her husband is addicted to pornography and has had multiple affairs. She begins to travel on the shame train. She questions why she is not good enough or pretty enough. She moves from immense hurt to anger, then bitterness and depression, and then finds herself on the fast track down the performance street. She begins to be obsessed with her weight, her body, her clothes, her make-up, her hairstyle, and her sensuality. The confusion over who she really is begins a cycle of depression and performance that is never-ending. This is the path where shame can take us. It is an intense stronghold, and it leads to other strongholds that keep us imprisoned.

Consider how men are conditioned by this world. "Big boys don't cry," "I must control my own destiny," "If we have good sex, we must have a good marriage!" "If I am a good provider for my family, that makes me a good husband." These lies only lead to emptiness in a relationship. A husband who is driven toward climbing the corporate ladder to be a great provider—the captain of his own ship—may be harsh at home. He attempts to connect only physically with his wife. The wife who is now feeling emotionally empty doesn't respond the way he wants. He feels hurt, which eventually leads to anger, bitterness, and possibly depression. The husband selfishly responds by either performing his way to reconnecting or stonewalling, manipulating his wife through the cold shoulder tactic, lashing out in anger, or causing destruction.

The root of his behavior is, "Because of my unmet need, I want you to hurt as badly as I do." Destruction occurs, the couple is separated emotionally, and the shame in the relationship rises to new heights. It's amazing how self-centered we can be, operating with an "If you don't meet my needs, I'll punish you" mentality.

Are You on the Shame Train?

If you experience shame, you may be in one of three places:

- Maybe you are aware that you have shame in your life, but you are unaware of the extent of your wounds.
- Or you may recognize the origin of your shame and are on the road toward healing.
- Or you may be walking in victory over your shame, carrying nothing but scars from the pain that you endured in your past.

Wherever you are, you can be assured that God desires peace for you, not confusion. As 1 Corinthians 14:33 says, "For God is not a God of disorder but of peace."

When we first began to share our testimony at various churches, we would get extremely emotional as we proclaimed the gut-wrenching truths of what our lives had become. We were humbled, sometimes embarrassed, and even scared of how people would receive our painful story. However, the more we shared and saw God using our pain to help others, the easier it became to visit the hurt. Now we can share our scars openly. They aren't nearly as painful as the initial wounds, and God continues to use them to minister to hurting couples. That is the God we serve. He loves to take broken and marred vessels and use them to bring honor and glory to Himself. If we were perfect, unscarred vessels, we could do life apart from Him. Being marred and scarred, there is no doubt that God's hand is at work in and through us to bring Him glory.

When we look at the perfect example of our Savior, we see that it is because of His stripes and scars that we are healed. His scars are for our healing. Isaiah 53:3–5 tells us His scars saved us from our sin. Others who share their scars hope to save others from making the same mistakes that they have made. But we also have to look at John 20:24–29. There we see that Jesus shared His scars with others so that they would believe. He offered comfort, courage, and hope to those who were walking in the shame of their sin. His scars set us free from our sin. The price was paid. Today His scars are still being shared with all who will listen.

You see, friend, what the enemy intends for evil, God turns to good (Genesis 50:20). The scars in your life, whether self-inflicted or not, are not purposed to condemn you. They are not present for you to feel like you have no value or are unacceptable, unapproved of, and unloved. God's Word says that there is no condemnation for those who are in Christ Jesus (Romans 8:1). Instead, our scars are purposed to comfort others. God wants us to share our scars. Following His example, we are to give others comfort, courage, and hope. In 2 Corinthians 1:3–5 we read, "Praise be to the God and Father of our Lord Jesus Christ, the Father of compassion and the God of all comfort, who comforts us in all our troubles, so that we can comfort those in any trouble with the comfort we ourselves have received from God."

Through our ministry, we have the privilege of meeting many of God's precious children. About two years ago, we received the opportunity to begin encouraging a couple whose marriage was being torn apart due to an extramarital affair. We watched the woman go through pain, anger, frustration, hatred, revenge, depression, and more. She was deteriorating physically, emotionally, and spiritually right before our eyes. But God pulled this precious girl back up and set her feet firmly on the solid rock of her Savior. She and her marriage were healed by the pure grace of God. With new understanding, she experienced the reality of Psalm 40:1–3:

"I waited patiently for the LORD;
    he turned to me and heard my cry.
He lifted me out of the slimy pit,
    out of the mud and mire;
he set my feet on a rock
    and gave me a firm place to stand.
He put a new song in my mouth,
    a hymn of praise to our God.
Many will see and fear and put their trust in the LORD."

Two years later, this same woman called us. The change in her voice was evidence enough that the Spirit had healed her and was controlling her life. In our conversation, she began to share the road of shame that the enemy took her down and how quickly she spiraled down to her defeat and his victory. Then she shared how Jesus had allowed her to understand the enemy's tactics. Miraculously, God set her free from the bondage of shame. When asked what caused the release from the shame, she said that she heard from an old friend who was going through a similar situation. She said that she was able to encourage and help her friend to walk through the hardest time in her life. She then told us that she would have never known how to help that woman had she not gone through it two years prior. At that moment God changed her heart and brought her to this conclusion: "My suffering can be used for somebody else's sake."

Oh friend, do you see? Sovereign God wants us to share our scars in order to proclaim His mercy, His grace, His goodness, and His unfailing, never-ending, unconditional love. When we allow the Holy Spirit to change our perspective about our sin from shame to scars, He allows our scars to comfort another.

Getting Off the Train

While sharing our pain certainly provides a healing balm to our shame, there is another integral step in the healing process. We need to cleanse ourselves from the sin that caused the shame. If it was your sin that caused your shame, you must forgive yourself and allow Christ to forgive you.

Have you repented and accepted the forgiveness of God, provided through the shed blood of His only Son, Jesus Christ? It is available to you, a free gift of grace, if you will ask. 1 John 1:7 says, "But if we walk in the light, as he is in the light, we have fellowship with one another, and the blood of Jesus, his Son, purifies us from all sin." Are there people keeping your past sins alive? Are there people who you know will consider themselves judge and jury over you for the rest of your life? Should anyone ever choose to judge you because of your past, understand this: they are really not questioning you, they're questioning the power of the blood of Jesus Christ. And if we as a people choose to cast stones at others' sin and shame, then we are making a mockery of the blood of Jesus. You go to God with your shame and confess your sin. Accept His cleansing, covering blood, and walk away in freedom.

Finally, if the shame is from someone else's sin, give it back to them. You took someone's shame that didn't belong to you. So many times we take other people's sin and shame on ourselves and accept it as our own, when it was never ours to begin with. Release the shame to its rightful owner.

As you journey toward healing and freedom, you will walk into a new dimension that you never dreamed of: the freedom of forgiveness. For some, *forgiveness* is not a word they can say, much less put into practice. The truth is, though, that a time will come when you are so healed and freed from your past, that you learn not only to forgive yourself, but you learn to forgive your perpetrator, even though you will never hear the words "I'm sorry" from them. Sound foreign to you?

We can tell you that we have seen many people locked in someone else's shame. Many have been physically assaulted by another. They feel so guilty and ashamed of the incident that it begins to eat them up like a cancer. The perpetrator may feel no remorse at all, while the victim is withering on the vine.

We witnessed this firsthand when we saw a little lady sitting alone in the corner of a conference center where we had spoken. She was frail, weak, and looked near death. We spoke with her and found that she had had many years of marriage struggles. But the root of the problem was an event that struck their home years before. A man forced his way inside their house and raped this woman. This precious little lady had held onto this shameful experience for many, many years until it had debilitated her beyond comprehension.

As we continued to speak with her, we shared with her the goodness that would come from her sharing her pain with us. We also encouraged her to continue to share it with others to comfort them. We then began to discuss the fact that the sin was not hers to bear, but was to be released to the one who had shamed her. From there, we talked about the forgiveness of God and how we must accept His forgiveness and then bestow it on others. With a startled expression, the woman asked us, "Are you telling me that I have to forgive that man for what he did to me?"

After a long pause, our answer rang loudly, "Yes, ma'am, you do." Fear, anger, frustration, and pain oozed from the heart of this dear sweet woman of God. We prayed and then headed for home.

When we reached Birmingham, we began to pray for this woman and her husband. We prayed that God would give her husband wisdom to come alongside and love his wife through this time. We prayed that he would be tender toward her. And we prayed that she would be released from her shame. Within a few weeks, we received a phone call at our home. We did not recognize the voice, but it was this dear, sweet lady. She sounded so different, so free. She told us that she had forgiven herself, had accepted the forgiveness of God, and forgiven the man who hurt her. She shared that she did not forgive the person because he deserved it, nor to exonerate him from his sin. Instead, she chose to forgive him for herself, so that she could be released from the shame she had carried around for so long—shame that wasn't hers to bear. She was obeying God because He told her to forgive. God had restored her joy, her life, and her home.

Are you traveling down the shame train? Are you in bondage to your sin or another's sin? Is shame keeping you from the joyous life God planned for you? There is freedom waiting for you, just around the corner, at the cross. Lay down your shame today. Determine that sin and shame no longer have a place in your life. The blood of Jesus has covered you, and Satan has no place to accuse you anymore. Revelation 12:11 says, "They overcame him

[Satan] by the blood of the Lamb and by the word of their testimony."

Share your scars, my friend. Tell others that there is hope. Set yourself free from the prison that sin has held you shackled in for so long. Embrace the forgiveness of God. It truly is the most freeing thing you will ever do.

Chapter Six

Learning to Love

any marriages have been damaged by the "it's all about me" attitude. It is an attitude that rules and reigns when husbands and wives focus on themselves and their individual needs. Manipulation of the other is almost always the result. When will we learn to love?

Scripture clearly calls all believers to ministry. As Christians, we often share the love of God with others, but within the walls of our homes, we have lost this passion. We don't view our marriages as ministry opportunities. Instead we focus on our own neediness and selfish wants. Seeking wholeness apart from God, we manipulate one another in alarming ways to get our needs met.

In this chapter, let's focus on the Bible book of 1 Corinthians, chapter 13. The love chapter, as it is commonly called, will be our foundational Scripture for love and ministry within marriage. Through the guidance of the Holy Spirit, may manipulation and selfishness be revealed and crucified in your relationship.

Love—we use this word with such carelessness. We love so many things. We love to play sports, we love our cars, our careers, our things. We love certain activities, certain foods, and certain relationships. Our fleshly nature is often driven by our feelings and responses, when in fact love is so much more than a feeling. Love involves commitment, determination, and dedication. It is a choice to love someone. Love is commanded by God, with clear instruction on how we should love and why we should love. In 1 Corinthians 13, God gives us a clear, concise, and detailed description of *agape* love (unconditional, godly love) as the benchmark of the love husbands and wives can share with one another. Consider these four verses:

"Love is patient, love is kind and is not jealous;
love does not brag and is not arrogant,
does not act unbecomingly;
it does not seek its own, is not provoked,
does not take into account a wrong suffered,
does not rejoice in unrighteousness, but rejoices
     with the truth;
bears all things, believes all things, hopes all things,
     endures all things.
Love never fails."
—1 Corinthians 13:4–8*a* NASB

As Jena and I have reflected on our marriage and the baggage we brought into the relationship, is it any wonder that we battled instead of ministering? Our road of reconciliation has been paved with the conscious decision and commitment to apply the calling of ministry in our marriage. In marriage you will be constantly faced with what we call "you or me" choices. The chart below summarizes and expands the descriptive qualities of love as found in 1 Corinthians 13.

LOVE IS	LOVE IS NOT
patient	impatient
kind	unkind
content	envious or jealous
humble	bragging, proud
not arrogant	puffed up, conceited or arrogant
decent, moral, and mannerly	indecent, ill mannered, rude
unselfish, with a servant's heart	selfish, self-seeking
even-tempered, calm	seeking to irritate, angry, sharp tempered
forgiving	unforgiving, revengeful
righteous, doing right by others	sinful, unrighteous, hurtful
truthful	deceitful, dishonest
covering, enduring, confidential	undependable, unreliable, unsafe
faithful, believing the good first	untrusting, pointing out the negative
hoping, encouraging, exhorting	skeptical, putting down, undermining
enduring all things	quitting
never failing, standing in support	cowardly, faithless

But how do these qualities really show up in our marriages? The practical, real-life examples that follow will clearly show how Jena and I manipulated one another. Keep in mind the deep-rooted needs of intimacy and importance, combined with a backdrop of experience that comes from our family of origin. All these dynamics, our personal propensity for selfishness, and the fact that no one ever explained any of this to us in the first place—much less taught us how to be husbands and wives—led us many times to act on our most primitive instincts.

The good news is this: today, you can make a conscious decision to become a minister in your marriage, just as Jena and I have become. This won't be easy. We have been trained to be manipulators. We have learned this at an early age.

When our daughter Jorja was 18 months old, she loved strawberry milk. It was a nightly ritual at our house for her to have a glass sometime before bed. One particular evening, Jorja asked for her milk, but we didn't have any. As we explained to her that we wouldn't be able to fix her a glass, she looked directly at me (Dale) and began to wink, smile, and show physical affection. Our son Cole looked at Jena and said, "Watch this, Dad's gonna go get her some milk!" Sure enough, I left at 10:30 P.M., drove to the grocery store, and bought the milk and strawberry syrup so Jorja could have her way.

Selfishness and a need for personal satisfaction is happening in marriages constantly. Manipulation occurs when a husband and wife, while they are full-grown adults, act like children in big people's bodies. As you follow along, we pray that you will see areas in your lives that need to change. We pray you will go from a selfish perspective to a ministry perspective. After all, Christ clearly says that we must decrease so that He can increase. If we want to save our lives, we must lose them, and when we are weak, He is strong. God gives grace to the humble, and our attitude should be the same as Christ as He humbly became a servant. Are you ready to learn how to love? That is the question.

Love Is Patient

In other words, love is long-suffering. The original form of the Greek word, *makrothumeo*, implies forbearance, endurance, with mildness and without resentment or indignation. In our home the struggle with patience showed up this way. Since I have a deep desire to feel important, I wanted to be on time to church, showing everybody that I had it all together. But Sundays were often frantic and furious—we woke up late, had children to get ready, and had to prepare for our church duties. For the first eight years of marriage, I would sit in the lounge chair and read the paper while Jena scurried about with the morning duties. When it was time to go, I grew impatient and began yelling, jingling my keys, and honking the car horn. Jena's and my tempers would flare, and then we would ride to church in silence, supposedly prepared for ministry and worship. Meanwhile resentment and indignation grew against one another. I attempted to control my family—thinking that demonstrated my importance—through my own impatience.

Impatience was also a problem when our expectations weren't met. Jena had in her mind the kind of spiritual journey I should be on. Many times she criticized me for not praying enough, not reading my Bible enough, or not leading the family the way she thought I should. She was impatient with my spiritual growth. Many a wife's intentions may be good, and some of the facts true, but because a man's deep desire is to feel important, the constant sense of failure causes him to retaliate or quit trying. Being impatient with your spouse can create problems. Now we join together in partnership. We are patient with the journey God has for each of us. We work together to get the kids ready for church, and we realize that as individuals, we don't always approach and handle things the same way, and that's okay. We don't nag and demand, but we demonstrate patience, one to the other, with long-suffering, mildness, and endurance. We love intently by praying for and being patient with each other.

Love Is Kind

Our family has taken many trips to Wal-Mart. On one of these ventures, we got out of the car and approached the entrance right behind an elderly woman. When she dropped her keys, I immediately bent down and retrieved them for her. When I did, she flowered me with accolades, compliments, and encouragement. The thank-yous were numerous. I showed her that chivalry was not dead. As Jena and the kids walked through the store, they noticed how proudly I walked, strutting around after performing such a good deed. When we went to checkout, Jena reached into her purse, pulled out her checkbook, and dropped her keys. As the knight in shining armor by her side, I said, "Hey Jena, you dropped your keys."

Where did the kindness go? Why was I so kind to a woman I didn't know but not to Jena? We thought about this later and realized some truths that gave us a new perspective on our marriage. First, Jena expected me to pick up her keys; after all, I had just done it for a stranger. Second, I didn't pick up her keys because I took her for granted, knowing that she was quite capable of picking them up herself. Third, I perceived my "ministry field" with the wrong perspective. I wasn't considering my marriage as a place of ministry.

We view our children, our church, our friendships, and even the perfect stranger at Wal-Mart as our ministry field, yet God has called us to minister to our mates first. The Bible clearly states in 1 Timothy 3:5 that a man cannot manage the things of God if he cannot manage his own home. The sad truth in marriages today is that we are more patient and kind to perfect strangers and friends than we are to our own mates. When we don't get our needs met, we say and do very unkind things to force our spouse to respond to us. This is neediness and manipulation in its purest form.

To be kind in marriage is to be gentle in behavior, courteous, and obliging. It carries the picture of outstretched arms and open hands to show favor, blessings, and honor to the mate God has given you. Now that's ministering through kindness. Ephesians 4:32 says, "Be kind and compassionate to one another, forgiving each other, just as in Christ God forgave you." We asked an elderly couple who attended one of our conferences the secret to their 50-plus years of marriage, and they both answered, "We just learned to be kind to one another." Kindness goes a long way in preserving a marriage.

Love Is Content

Jealousy and envy showed up in our marriage when I felt like Jena was more "important" than I was. We remember a specific time when Jena was leading a women's retreat, and the people in attendance were changed by the message that God had given her. As these women kept coming to me with praise of how God moved and what a wonderful job Jena did in leadership, I found myself envious of her glory. I turned Jena's good attributes, accomplishments, and achievements into a source of contention, because I couldn't handle her getting more credit than I did.

We have had many couples sit and talk with us, where one spouse or sometimes both would say, "My spouse just doesn't support me," or "He won't let me have any friends," or "She won't let me lead Bible study," or "She knows I love to sing, but she refuses to support the gifts God has given me." We attempt to hold one another captive to our own neediness, refusing to be content with who we are. The truth is that we must all be content where God has us—anything good comes from God anyway. We had nothing to do with it and He will not share His Glory with another.

Learning to love in your marriage means you are not jealous. Love is not grieved at the good of others—their gifts, qualities, positions, or prosperity in life. Loving through contentment is also being satisfied with your personal standard of living. Marriages often struggle because couples compare their own lives with the wealth and accomplishments of others. "Keeping up with the Joneses" can drive a wedge between a couple, as the pressure rises to acquire more and live outside your means, instead of being content with what God has provided. It would be a great display of love to look at your spouse and clearly communicate that you love them just the way they are, and you are content with where you are together as Christ continues to grow you in your life. This doesn't mean you don't strive to improve, but rather you are content while ever striving.

Love Is Humble

Love does not brag or vaunt itself; rather it honors and prefers one another (Romans 12:10). Loving through humility requires that you take the position described in Philippians chapter 2, where we are to have the same attitude as Christ Jesus. Manipulation shows up when couples, in the heat of an argument, begin stacking their decks. In the midst of conflict, we operate out of the principle that "he who has the most cards in his deck, wins!" So we stack our decks by such statements as, "I always do this and this and this . . . and you don't do anything." The stacking language of "I always," and "you never," builds us up to a higher position, somehow gaining what we perceive to be leverage in the battle. The reality is that this is all about you bragging on you, and not you humbly loving your mate.

Love Is Not Arrogant

This quality of love carries the above reference to humility much deeper. While we are to be humble and not brag, criticism through arrogance carries with it a completely different scheme. The action here consists of pride and conceit. Pride cometh before a fall, and God says that He hates it. We emotionally attempt to control our spouses with pride, arrogance, and conceit by thinking that we "know it all." We think we are right all the time and often shame our spouse into feelings of worthlessness. We are too proud to say we are sorry when we know we are wrong. We are too conceited to admit that we have hurt one another, so we stonewall, pout, and give the cold-shoulder instead of loving.

Arrogance also depicts an attitude that we know the minds, actions, and motives of our spouses. We make statements such as, "They've always been that way, and they always will be, there's no changing them." Husbands and wives should strive not to be "puffed up" but modest, allowing change to occur by the Spirit of God working in their spouse, understanding this is God's job to change their spouse, and not theirs. A loving husband or wife prays for their spouse and demonstrates godly characteristics in their own life that will demonstrate to their mate the very qualities of Christ. It means, *I will not be conceited or demand my own way all of the time.* Loving your spouse without arrogance is God's command.

Love Is Decent, Moral, and Mannerly

Love does not behave in an unbecoming or unseemly way. The Greek word *aschemoneo*, used in 1 Corinthians 13:5, speaks of defying a moral and mannerly standard. Love is not rude or ill mannered. During the early years of our marriage, I loved to tell jokes at Jena's expense. While you may not think of this as indecent, the reality is that it was dishonoring and rude behavior toward her. The root of the issue was my need to feel important. When my friends laughed and thought I was funny, I felt important. But it is not loving to treat our spouses with disrespect.

We have had many couples, men and women alike, who have shared with us that their spouse makes them feel stupid and minimizes their feelings instead of validating them. Decent, moral, and mannerly love carries with it common courtesy. Often when we have guests in our home, the pleases, thank-yous, and compliments fill the air. Yet when we are at home alone we suddenly treat each other with an entirely different set of rules. In other words, we are not using our manners. Loving one another in the marriage relationship means you should never be embarrassing, unbecoming, or unseemly at the expense of your mate. It requires respect for one another and choosing to hold your spouse before others in high regard.

Love Is Unselfish

The selfish heart is at the core of all marital struggles. If it were not for selfishness, the divorce rate in this country would be basically non-existent. Selfishness drives all of us, at some time. Isaiah 53:6 says, "We all, like sheep, have gone astray, each of us has turned to his own way." Let's face it, we are selfish because of our sin nature. Yet God has given us new life through Christ: "the old has gone, the new has come!" We are to be transformed into His image, becoming more like Him, and less like us. God commands us to love our neighbors, even our spouses first, as ourselves.

Here's the problem. Because we are selfish, we tend to love ourselves more than we do our spouses. We disobey God because we'd rather have our own needs met. We want our way, on our timetable. Unselfish love, however, commands that we constantly ask, "How can I serve my spouse today?" This does not mean that you become a doormat, that everything is one-sided, or you get taken advantage of, but rather you become "givers" more than "takers." If both spouses operate from a "giver" perspective rather than a "taker" perspective, love transforms their home.

Love Is Even-Tempered

Anger, hot-temperedness, being easily provoked, being irritating, and threatening are all forms of control in marriage. Yet 1 Corinthians commands that our love be demonstrated by being even-tempered. Being angry and hot-tempered is a serious problem in marriages today. At the heart of anger is hurt—our neediness and expectations are unfulfilled, so we vent. Our spouse has done or said something that hurt us, so we lash out in anger.

In our marriage, it showed up like this: Jena would have a deep need to be encouraged emotionally. She wanted me to verbally affirm her—tell her how much

I loved her and encourage her in her walk with the Lord. Yet when I didn't, or didn't the way Jena expected me to, she became demanding. Because I (like most people) don't like to fail, I responded in anger, hoping that Jena would stop being so demanding. I thought my apparent anger would stop Jena from criticizing. In fact, neither of us was having our needs met. Our intimacy was broken down by our demanding spirits, controlling attitudes, and anger. This is not God's plan for loving one another. Loving your spouse in ways as described in 1 Corinthians 13 means that you make decisions that soften and do not irritate your husband or wife. You demonstrate love to your spouse in a manner that stimulates positive responses and calming attitudes.

Love Is Forgiving

We'll discuss authentic forgiveness thoroughly in Chapter 8. Yet for our discussion in this chapter we need to point out that learning to love is demonstrated through true God-like forgiveness. Very simply, love does not keep a record of wrongs. We remember many arguments in the early days of our marriage, when in the heat of the battle, one or both of us would bring up something that happened months or even years before. We would be right in the middle of a disagreement, and Jena would say, "I remember in 1984, when you said that my hair looked stupid!" I would respond, "Well, I remember in 1984 when you forgot my birthday present!" We keep these records of wrongs, or our ledger of debits and credits, just in case we need them in the future.

The fact of the matter is that most of us cash in our credits and we keep the debits as a weapon to use later. Bringing up past hurt and pain, when these should have been forgiven, is not love. The motive behind our behavior is that we want our spouse to hurt as much as they hurt us. This is a revengeful attitude, and not love. Love is found when you and your spouse understand the amount of forgiveness you have received from Christ. Then through ministry to one another, offer that same forgiveness by demonstrating mercy and grace to your partner.

Love Is Righteous

Love does right by others. It doesn't seek to hurt them physically, mentally, spiritually, or emotionally. Our love for our spouses should be so rich and genuine that it is righteous by its very nature. So what is righteousness? It is to be right with God. How can you have righteous love for your spouse? The Bible says that no one is righteous, no not one, and that all have sinned and fallen short of the glory of God. Yet while we were yet sinners, Christ died for us.

It is not our own righteousness that we are speaking of, but rather the righteousness of God. The righteousness of God that comes into a person's life changes them. It is the gift of Christ that makes us righteous. And when you accept Christ into your life, you are placed into a position of righteousness because of Jesus Christ. We become right with God through Jesus Christ. In marriage we show that we are right with God by the way we treat our husband or wife. When we demonstrate the character of Christ through righteous love, we are committed to love them the way Christ loves.

Love Is Truthful

Marital breakdown occurs in a marriage when deceit and dishonesty rule. It would occur in our marriage when we would have conversations about upcoming events or plans for the weekend. I'd only tell Jena the "necessary" information. As an example, one Thursday night we were sitting in the den, talking about what we'd be doing that weekend. I knew I had a tee-time on the golf course on Sunday afternoon, but failed to mention it to Jena. Instead, we made plans for what we'd do together on Saturday. Saturday night I said "Oh, Jena, by the way, I have a tee-time tomorrow at 1:30." Jena responded, "We've been together all day, why are you just mentioning this now? Why didn't you tell me about this Thursday night when we were discussing the plans for the weekend? What else are you not telling me?" Trust started to break down between us.

It would also happen when Jena knew she wanted to have a night out with the girls. As we would discuss our plans, the night out would be downplayed as, "By the way, some girls and I are gonna go to the movies tonight. You don't mind do you?" Jena had known about this night out for days, but failed to be completely truthful because she didn't want me to object. Many couples communicate with the attitude of "what they don't know won't hurt them!" or "I tell my spouse on a 'need to know basis.'"

Truthful love in marriage compels us to be honest and forthright. Love rejoices in the truth. This truth is so much more, however, than just sharing facts and plans. Loving through truth is about character as you demonstrate a lifestyle of truth and honesty in your marriage. Loving truth rejoices when you as a couple are grounded in the application and expression of God's truth, His Word, in your life. Loving truth is powerful in marriage when we allow God's Word to conquer and overcome our sinful nature. When we walk in obedience to God's Word, our lives and our marriages are conformed into accurate representations of His truth living in our hearts and homes. Truthful love in marriage understands that without truth, trust is lost.

Love Bears All Things

The Greek word *stego*, used in 1 Corinthians 13:7, means to cover as a roof, or to patiently endure, to put up with. When a storm comes, you naturally head for cover. You patiently endure the rain under some form of shelter until the rain subsides. So it is with marriage. The struggles and stresses of life are going to come like a storm approaching your home. Rather than running to the quickest way out, God desires for us to patiently endure while running together under His umbrella of protection until the struggle subsides. Godlike love bears all things. Learning to "endure" or "put up with" one another's weak points creates marriage partners of grace. This does not mean we settle for second best, it simply means we are to love in such a way that we bear all things with one another, bestow grace to our mates, and allow them to grow and change into the person Christ wants them to become. Growing, godly couples love one another by bearing all things and weathering the storms of life.

Love Believes All Things

Our fleshly nature and selfish attitudes often cause us to be skeptics—untrusting of others. Of course, this occurs because many marriages live in past hurt instead of present hope. We hang onto the moments of past failures and disappointments. Jena and I remember vividly in our marriage, especially in the days of our heated battles and arguments, that we believed the negative about the other rather than the positive. In the middle of our divorce proceedings, it was very common for Jena to make statements such as, "I've heard it all before. Your words mean nothing to me. You can't give me one good reason to stay married to you!" I responded, "You talk a good game, but I don't believe a word you say." These cutting, critical statements would drive a wedge deeply between us.

Yet love in marriage should believe all things. You choose to believe the best of your spouse, trusting them until they give you a reason not to. It means the direction of your will is to seek the positive rather than the negative. It means that you love one another by looking for the best, seeking ways to encourage and exhort. It is a conscious decision to love by hoping for the best while giving the benefit of the doubt.

Love Hopes All Things

Hope in love is powerful! Many couples today are struggling because they feel their marriage is hopeless. We certainly did. Yet we know from firsthand experience that there is always hope with Jesus. He is the giver of hope and is capable of restoring the most hopeless relationship. We remember the day we started our journey toward reconciliation. We asked ourselves, *Is this possible? Can we do this? Is this hopeless?* As we journeyed through the uncharted waters, it was our hope in Christ that carried us through. As Christ continued to reveal Himself as faithful and true, our hope in one another, through Christ, began to take on an entirely new focus. As we witnessed Christ changing us, we moved from a hopeless situation to a hope-filled relationship. When we approached our reconciliation with the power of having hope in Jesus and then one another,

Christ restored all the love, and so much more that had been lost.

It was a faith moment for us. Did we truly believe in the power of God to restore and renew? Could we lay down our selfish, hopeless perspectives and live out the principle that the love of Christ hopes for all things? "Now these three remain: faith, hope and love. But the greatest of these is love" (1 Corinthians 13:13). As faith in God strengthens, hope showers down. It is this hope, the hope of glory, that catapults us to God-like love.

Love Endures All Things

In 1 Corinthians 13:7, the Greek word for endure, *hupomeno*, means to remain, to have fortitude, and to persevere. You may be facing the most difficult time in your marriage. You may have raised your children and found out that your marriage is now empty because the house is empty. You may have been let down, hurt, disappointed, betrayed, and facing many trials and troubles. There were many days for Jena and me that our flesh cried out for us to walk away, give up, and quit. Since our divorce and remarriage, we have realized how weak our love really was.

Oh, friend, walking away and quitting is not the answer. We want to impress upon you to stand your ground and endure, because of Christ's love for you. Enduring love understands that regardless of the response or lack of response, rejection or embracing actions and attitudes of my spouse, I am going to behave with integrity and in the right manner. It means that I am responsible for making sure my behavior is godly. Sometimes my spouse is not lovable, but I am going to endure and love them anyway. Sometimes they reject me and remain distant, but I am going to continue to pursue and love them.

Sometimes my spouse simply won't receive my actions and attempts, yet I understand that enduring love is more about giving than receiving. In fact, I am doing the right thing out of obedience to Christ, because of my love for Him. Christ's love for me endured all the way to the cross. Therefore I must live a life of enduring love, understanding that this kind of love changes hearts and lives.

However, let us be clear that enduring love does not mean you allow abusive situations to continue. Sin carries consequences, and love never helps someone sin. The highest level of enduring love would be to set appropriate boundaries for your sponse, so that godly, Christlike love can be developed.

Love Never Fails

Do you really believe that love never fails? Are you so consumed by your own needs and fears that you are afraid that your love will fail? Is your marriage failing? Is your relationship with your spouse empty and bankrupt? Is it even possible that your love for one another can return? All of these are valid questions that we faced. Our hearts' desire is to communicate that a godly marriage is available to each and every one of us. We know that applying the principles of 1 Corinthians 13 works. It teaches us to love the way God intended us to love. That kind of love never fails. His Word is true; you can count on it. But will you choose to love, regardless? It is a matter of obedience to His Word that enables you to find yourself on the ministry side of love.

As we conclude, take another moment and look at the chart at the front of this chapter. Where do you find yourself as you are learning to love? Are you demonstrating the sixteen qualities of *agape* love to your mate? Can you replace the word "love" with your name in the Scripture? This is to be our goal. When you can honestly do this, you are truly loving your mate. Will you dedicate yourself to loving your spouse the way 1 Corinthians commands? Loving one another in this manner will transform marriages into the blessings they were created to be.

Chapter Seven

When Battle Lines Are Drawn

The longer we live, the more we realize the need for handling conflict in a Christlike manner. Conflict is a given—it is going to come. Where there is relationship, there are going to be battle lines at some point. Few of us enjoy conflict, so many of us don't handle it well. We must diligently search for God's desire for us in that conflict, a way to honor Him in the end.

Have you ever noticed that we live in a world where choices are innumerable? From ice cream flavors to the latest fashions, our world is filled with choices for us to make. Conflict comes with a set of choices all its own. Let's look at some possible choices.

Retreat

The first choice we have in the midst of conflict is to retreat. Many of us quickly withdraw and isolate ourselves when conflict comes up. When we think about retreating, the first Bible story that comes to mind is Jonah. God told him to head to Nineveh and to speak on His behalf (Jonah 1:2), yet Jonah chose to run away to Tarshish instead. Why do you think Jonah ran away? Many may believe it was because the city of Nineveh was a great city of 120,000 people (Jonah 4:11), and Jonah did not want to witness to them for fear that they would become more favorable to God than Jonah's people. Still others believe he was simply afraid that he would be killed for his witnessing. Whatever caused Jonah to retreat, fear played a major part.

Fear can be an enormous motivator because it has such an impact. Many times it controls what we do. When conflict emerges, we retreat in fear. We avoid the conflict at all costs to preserve our hearts from further pain. We also fear that we might have to admit our "wrongness" if we acknowledge the conflict, and then be held accountable to change. We certainly don't like to admit when we are wrong and we certainly don't want to have to change. Therefore, we retreat in a hasty manner.

If you learned as a child to keep peace at all costs, then you are probably conditioned to retreat. Also, if you avoided your parents when they had conflict, you are probably conditioned to retreat. You may choose to dive into all sorts of busyness to avoid dealing with it. The problem with retreating is this: when all of the busyness has subsided, the conflict is still there, as unresolved as it ever was.

We call those who choose to retreat *stuffers and spewers*. Those who retreat stuff their hurt, anger, and frustration into the depths of their souls, where it rots into bitterness. Often no one knows about the stuffer's hurt. They get angry because of others' indifference, but others are clueless. Others continue to hurt the stuffer because they have no idea they are doing it, and then the stuffer gets angrier and the vicious cycle rolls on. The stuffer thinks the conflict will go away if they can push it down deep enough for long enough. But much like a shaken Dr. Pepper, one incident, whether small or large, can "pop the cap" of your heart, and soon you find yourself spewing angry words like daggers to the heart. Because the stuffer avoided the conflict, this bitterness spews forth and does serious damage.

Rebel

If you are not one who retreats, you might be one who rebels. Rebelling in the midst of conflict is a choice you can make. Isaiah 53:6 says that we are a bunch of sheep who want to go our own way, while James 4:17 says, "Anyone, then, who knows the good he ought to do and doesn't do it, sins." Within all of us is the rebellious nature that knows what we are supposed to do, but we usually choose to do whatever suits our selfish nature. In conflict, there is no difference.

Why do we rebel? Why do we feel the need to dig our heels in and come out fighting? Because we want to be right. We don't want to have to admit that we are wrong. Therefore, we will blame the other for our behavior with words like, "Well, I would have never done this if you hadn't done that!" in hopes that they will accept all of the blame.

The problem is that a scenario like this results in one person taking all of the blame, while another is never held responsible for the part that they played. Thus, the rebellious person never has the conviction or sees the need for change in their behavior and the conflict and pain continues in the relationship. They remain the same in their ungodly behavior, because they have passed that off to another by justifying their actions. This is not beneficial for either party involved.

If you'll remember, we began this chapter with discussing choices. The truth is that many of us need to see that we choose our own behavior. We choose how we will respond and act in certain situations. Nobody chooses that for you. **Your spouse cannot "make" you do anything. Your sin is just that, your sin.**

Which brings us to the God-honoring choice that we must intentionally decide upon when the battle lines are drawn. And that is to choose personal responsibility. We must choose to take responsibility for ourselves and the ways in which we behave.

Responsibility

This never became so evident to us until we witnessed our children in a conflict. Jorja, age 4, was watching television.

Cole, our 7-year-old, came into the room and changed the channel, because he was not interested in "kiddie stuff." Now you need to know that Cole was always picking at Jorja and pushing her around because he thought older brothers could do that. He had also been fully warned by both of us that one day Jorja would grow up and would get him back for all of his physical meanness. A blood-curdling scream came from the den of our home. We discovered Jorja, grabbing Cole by the hair and pulling it so tightly that he was screaming out in total pain. When we arrived, Jorja had a great big smile on her face, so pleased by her ability to debilitate her brother.

After many I-told-you-sos, Jena proceeded to take Cole and Jorja over to the sofa to discuss the dynamics of their conflict. When she asked Cole what he did, his response was, "She pulled my hair!" Jena told Cole that she didn't ask what Jorja did, but rather what he did. He responded with the fact that he turned the channel while Jorja was watching her show. When Jorja was asked about the part she played in the conflict her answer was much the same, "Well, he changed the channel!" Isn't that just like us? We blame the other for our behavior, rarely admitting our part of the conflict.

At that moment, Jena began to discuss with Cole and Jorja their sin in the sight of God. She then asked Cole and Jorja to do a few things. They had to confess their sin, call it sin, and seek the other's forgiveness. Jorja was required to say, "Cole, I pulled your hair and it was wrong. It was sin. I am sorry. Will you forgive me?" They probably don't enjoy that little routine in our home, but our hopes are that they will learn early in life the value of taking responsibility for their own actions without blaming another.

In our society today, we do not call sin what it is. Oh, what our marriages, homes, churches, communities, and world would look like if we would just call sin what it really is, then confess, repent, and take personal responsibility for the part we play. If couples could just let this principle melt into their hearts, marriages would change dramatically. Just as our eternal destination depends on no one but us, so our behavior is to be owned by no one but us. We must choose to take responsibility for ourselves—the sin in our lives and relationships—and begin developing authentic, Christ-like love and forgiveness.

Love's Place in the Battle

Love. We've heard about it from all sorts of talk shows. We've seen it on television, the movies, and other areas of media. We dedicated an entire chapter (Chapter 6) to learning how to love. But what does love do when there is a battle going on inside your home? Too many couples have begun to operate in the world's definition of love instead of God's. Christ-like, agape, real love is the most fulfilling, beautiful part of the marriage relationship. First we have to know the lover of our souls, Jesus Christ, to ever truly understand love in its deepest and fullest form. Then we can authenticate His love to others.

Have you ever tried to fight with somebody who demonstrates love to you? You just can't do it! You can try to be mean or harsh or even serious, but when they are being kind to you, you just can't fight with them. If we are going to take responsibility for ourselves when it comes to conflict and battles, we have got to learn to exercise *agape* love with one another. If love is your motivation, then love will never fail, because God's Word promises us just that (1 Corinthians 13).

Agape is the Greek word for Christlike love. It means unconditional love, love that remains constant with no strings attached. It involves choosing to love, even though your spouse may be unloving or unlovable. It puts the other's interest ahead of your own. If you are allowing these traits of love to be manifested in your life, it is extremely unlikely that you will experience unresolved conflict. As you consciously make the choice to love, applying personal responsibility to your actions, then true authentic love will be characterized by the following four qualities found in God's Word.

Make Love a Priority

In Mark 4, Jesus is at the height of His ministry and yet the Jewish leaders are questioning His every move. Does your spouse question your every move? Do you question them in the same way? Jesus understands how that feels, and He responded with one thing: love. One of the rulers asked

Him this: "Out of all the commandments given, which is the most important?" Jesus' answer? Love.

Christ made love the priority of His life. Love was the motivation for everything He did and said. Can that be said of you? We are often motivated by a desire to win, to be right, to be heard, and to get our own way when conflict comes. Jesus Christ made love the heart of all that He was. It was priority for Him.

Can your spouse say that loving God and loving your family is priority for you? Have children, careers, and life taken priority over the place of love for your spouse? It doesn't have to.

We know a couple who are fellow sojourners in the Lord. They challenge us, inspire us, pray for us, and hold us accountable. When we first remarried, our challenge from them was to create a "priority time" to love each other through the gift of undivided attention. They challenged us to make time for each other every day to re-connect from our time apart.

We had that priority time at night after the children went to bed, while we watched *Andy Griffith* together! Our friends reminded us of this: if God wants us to teach our children what marriage looks like, but we reconnect after the children are asleep, then what kind of view are we giving our children of what a healthy, loving marriage looks like?

So now, as soon as Dale comes home from work, we tell our children, "It is time for mom and dad to have some time together. Please do not interrupt us unless you are dragging a bloody arm or leg behind you. Otherwise, we will let you know when we are finished." Then, we sit together in our den and discuss our days with one another. We talk about what happened in our day, how it made us feel, and what we need from each other for the rest of the evening.

That practice not only helps us reconnect for the rest of the evening, it shows us that we are more important to each other than anything else that might be pressing. It also greatly benefits our children because they see parents who put each other first, and they then learn the importance of love as a priority in their future marriage.

Just think for a moment about some typical, stressful days in your home. For us, I (Jena) would be cooking and Dale would walk in. Though I asked how Dale's day was, I was also trying to get Jorja to take her bath, answering questions from Cole about a project, and trying to answer the phone. Somewhere in that confusion, Dale headed to the recliner because he had no desire to compete for my attention. He had had a terrible day, and now the house was crazy too. So he went to escape into the chair. Then I would get mad at him for not helping me. After all, I had worked just as hard and my day wasn't over until the children were in bed, asleep. So I would walk upstairs with a basket of laundry and drop it at his feet. That made him mad. After all, he had worked all day long to provide for his family. The least we could do is give him a little appreciation. By the end of the evening, I was furious and not speaking to Dale, and Dale was infuriated for having to fold sheets. He gave me the "silent treatment."

Does this describe your house? This conflict would never have occurred if love had been a priority in our home. If I had stopped what I was doing and given Dale my undivided attention, I would have heard about his terrible day, my struggles could have been voiced, and we could understand how the other was feeling. Then we could have been encouragers for the rest of the evening. Making your love relationship a priority can make all the difference in the world, and your children will receive an accurate representation of what a God-honoring marriage looks like.

Commit to Each Other

God also showed His agape love for us by His commitment. Have you told your spouse that no matter what, you are committed? We shudder when we think of our society's view of commitment. When we leased a car not too long ago, we found out that it is easier to get out of a marriage than it is an automobile lease. People give you their word, and then back out because something came up or something better came along. Our promises are empty, our words cheap, and the enemy is rejoicing.

When I (Jena) was a child, I can remember picking one activity that I would participate in for the year. You can bet that if I made a commitment, my parents would see to it that I remained a faithful part of the team or class until the very last day. Why? Because they taught me the value of commitment.

But commitment today only seems to hold true if there is nothing better to do. Commitment only has to be followed when it feels good. As soon as the feelings go, commitment goes right along with it. Hear this one truth: While feelings are often important indicators of reality, they can also be deceiving. They can lead us away from the truth. Our feelings can swing us in all directions, tossing us to and fro with every wind of circumstance. We must be careful about allowing our feelings to determine our behavior and our responses. Properly processing your feelings and walking in truth is critical to marriage.

If parents only fed their children when they felt like it, there would be lots more starving kids in this world. If people only went to work when they felt like it, they probably wouldn't maintain their jobs for very long. And because people stay committed to their marriages only as long as the feelings are there, the divorce rate is soaring.

The world we live in tells us that when we feel, then we act, and when the feelings are gone, we stop the actions. God's Word explains the opposite. If we act like we love each other, then the feelings will come, but the commitment to obeying and trusting God through faith comes first.

What would it have been like if Christ had come to this earth, ministered just as He did, but then went to God and said, "Father, these people are good-for-nothings. I try and show them Your ways and they don't listen. They are a bunch of ungrateful people who do not deserve Your love. Therefore, I have decided not to pay the penalty for their sin." That is not what our Savor did. Our Savior looked mockery in the face and bore the sin of the world. He remained faithful and committed to the end. We are to do nothing less, and part of taking responsibility for yourself means that you love your spouse by committing yourself and your love to them forever, even when the feelings have faded. It also means that in the midst of a conflict, you remember that your spouse is not your enemy, but that you are on the same team and are committed to be at peace with one another.

Follow Through with Action

God demonstrated His love for us in that while we were sinners, He died for us (Romans 5:8). Love must also be demonstrated in your home, especially when conflict begins to arise. Have you ever made a comment to your spouse like this: "I shouldn't have to prove myself to you"? Well, let us tell you a secret: Yes you do. Jesus Christ spent much of His life proving the full extent of His love. He proved His love for us all the way to a cruel, rugged cross. We, too, must spend our lives proving our love for our Savior through obedience and proving our love for our spouses through demonstration.

Many of you may have attempted to demonstrate love, but have found that it was not received. Author and speaker Gary Chapman has written an incredible book called *The Five Love Languages*. This book is a must-read for anyone who wants to love their spouse, children, family, and friends in the ways that they can best receive and understand love. Dr. Chapman shares that there are five tangible ways that people give and receive love. If you are giving love to another person who does not recognize love in that way, then it is as if you are speaking another language to them.

When Dale and I began to recognize our love languages as well as our children's love languages, we were no longer spinning our wheels. We were actually loving others in a way that they could understand, and thus revitalizing our relationships. It was incredible to see our children respond because they were understanding in new ways the depths of their parents' love.

When our daughter, Jorja, was beginning school, she had a real struggle with separation. She made awful scenes in the school car line as she cried and begged not to have to go to school because she wanted to stay at home. I would cry all the way home, begging God to take care of Jorja. Dale offered to take Jorja to school to save me the tears, but he called after the first day crying too! At one point, we were considering paying someone to take our daughter to school! With a broken heart, I began to ask God to help our family survive this struggle, and to give us discernment as to what to do. In His still, small voice, the

Spirit of God whispered, "Spend time with Jorja." Well, I was a bit miffed at that statement. After all, I stayed home with the children and they were with me a lot of the time. But as I pondered this more and more, I realized that though Jorja was with me, she rarely got my complete attention. Jorja's way of receiving love was through spending time together.

The next afternoon, Jorja and I came home from school, grabbed a quick snack, and then went out to the trampoline and worked on Jorja's spelling together. It only took about 20 minutes, but the next day there were no more tears. The next evening at bedtime, I got under the covers with Jorja and read her a book with the flashlight. The next morning again, there were no tears. Jorja was no longer struggling with the anxieties of separation, because she was experiencing love in a way that she could receive it.

We must be demonstrators of our love for one another. When couples first fall in love, they constantly prove their love with all sorts of special gifts, words, and time. We must continue to show love to our spouses after marriage. When we demonstrate love to one another regularly, conflicts can be resolved in ways that will bear healthy, fulfilling fruit in our marriages.

Serve Each Other

The Greek word for servant is *doulos*. It is a word that implies someone who gives his or herself up to another's will, a slave, to be devoted to another as you disregard your own interest. Exodus 21:1–6 provides a clear parallel between servant and master.

"If you buy a Hebrew servant, he is to serve you for six years. But in the seventh year, he shall go free, without paying anything. If he comes alone, he is to go free alone; but if he has a wife when he comes, she is to go with him. If his master gives him a wife and she bears him sons or daughters, the woman and her children shall belong to her master, and only the man shall go free. But if the servant declares, 'I love my master and my wife and children and do not want to go free,' then his master must take him before the judges. He shall take him to the door or the doorpost and pierce his ear with an awl. Then he will be his servant for life."—Exodus 21:1–6

This passage of Scripture is rich with truths about love, servanthood, and marriage. The basis is the Hebrew servant. After he has served his master for seven years he is faced with the choice to remain a servant, or to go free. Wow, do we face these same choices everyday? We are constantly faced with choosing to whom we are loyal. As the passage continues to unfold, we see that the master, as the giver of the wife, retains the wife and children. What a beautiful scriptural picture of the gift of God, as He bestowed the blessing of a wife and children to a husband. We need to understand that we do not own our spouses, and as parents we do not own our children. Rather our mates and our children are gifts from God, entrusted to us for the nurture and care they deserve, just as God Himself has nurtured and cared for us. Couples have a great responsibility to honor one another as the true gift and blessing they are.

The turning point of this passage occurs in verse 5: "But if the servant declares, I love . . . ." Love demands servanthood. The slave can go free, but because of love he remains. Who is his love and dedication to? Is it the wife and children? Yes, but it starts with his master. In fact, it is the love for the master that causes the slave to experience the pain of being marked. The custom was to take the slave to the doorpost and pierce his ear with an awl, so that everyone who looked upon him would know that he was a *doulos*, a servant for his master. Why is this so important for marriages today? Because when a couple is sold out to Christ, and their love is grounded by a servant's dedication to Christ and one another, their marriage will have a "marked" difference. In other words, their marriage will be different, because Christ has made a difference.

Servanthood in marriage—when a husband and wife put each other before themselves—marks them as children of God. When someone looks at your marriage, they should notice a difference in how you live your life, how you treat your spouse, how you show love one to another. Servanthood is a visible characteristic of love, when Christ is the catalyst to serve.

This is precisely what Christ demonstrated as he loved us all the way to the cross of Calvary. Philippians 2:1–7 provides us with the depth of Christ love and servant's heart.

"If you have any encouragement from being united with Christ, if any comfort from his love, if any fellowship with the Spirit, if any tenderness and compassion, then make my joy complete by being like-minded, having the same love, being one in spirit and purpose. Do nothing out of selfish ambition or vain conceit, but in humility consider others better than yourselves. Each of you should look not only to your own interests, but also to the interests of others. Your attitude should be the same as that of Christ Jesus: Who, being in very nature God, did not consider equality with God something to be grasped, but made himself nothing, taking the very nature of a servant, being made in human likeness. —Philippians 2:1–7

Christ is the epitome of a servant. The passage beckons us all to join Him in His call to love one another, fully. The passage provides us with some clear commands, and blessings, if we will humble ourselves under God and become a servant. We are called to make joy complete as we love. We are called to unity. We are challenged to do nothing out of selfish ambition or personal gain, but be humble. Our attitude and our minds should align with Christ as we see His character outlined before us: Christ was fully God, fully man. He submitted and aligned His will to His heavenly Father, not desiring to grasp equality but emptied

Himself of everything, taking the very nature of a servant, a *doulos* for His heavenly Father.

Yet unlike the servant of Exodus 21, Christ did not get His ear pierced. He was pierced for our transgressions by the nails of a cruel cross. His servant's heart carried Him all the way to Calvary. More than 2000 years ago, the world was shown what it really means to be a servant.

"And being found in appearance as a man, he humbled himself and became obedient to death—even death on a cross! Therefore God exalted him to the highest place and gave him the name that is above every name, that at the name of Jesus every knee should bow, in heaven and on earth and under the earth, and every tongue confess that Jesus Christ is Lord, to the glory of God the Father."
—Philippians 2:8–11

Will you continue to retreat because of fear and lack of faith? Will you rebel, making others hurt just as much as you have, or will you choose to take personal responsibility for your actions, and begin to demonstrate the four characteristics of authentic love? The beauty of a choice is you get to make one. You can continue to operate and act in the fleshly ways that have become so natural, or you can choose to love.

The road of healing, reconciliation, and hope in our marriage began as we committed ourselves to take personal responsibility for what we had done. We committed ourselves to God to love by making one another a priority. We committed to love regardless of the faded feelings, as we put love into action and became a servant. Authentic *agape* love requires nothing less. Priority, commitment, action, servanthood. When we did this, God allowed our marriage to sing with the psalmist:

"I waited patiently for the LORD;
　　he turned to me and heard my cry.
He lifted me out of the slimy pit,
　　out of the mud and mire;
he set my feet on a rock
　　and gave me a firm place to stand.
He put a new song in my mouth,
　　a hymn of praise to our God.
Many will see and fear and put their trust in the LORD."
—Psalm 40:1–3

When the battle lines are drawn, will you retreat, rebel, or take personal responsibility through authentic love? The choice is yours.

Chapter Eight

Authentic Forgiveness

C onflict often causes damage. Maybe you have realized that in the past. You might be suffering the consequences now of conflict that wasn't handled in a godly manner years ago. Don't despair. There is hope. There is a solution. It's called *forgiveness*.

In this chapter we'll focus on authentic forgiveness—what it requires and what it looks like in a marriage (or any relationship for that matter). As a couple, we had a serious problem understanding true forgiveness. We bought into what the world says about forgiveness but not what God says; they are vastly different. Not until we experienced our divorce and remarriage did we understand how deeply we had been forgiven. Not forgiven by each other necessarily, but forgiven by Christ first. If you are not a believer, and you have never accepted the forgiveness of Christ for your sins, then you will never be able to truly forgive others. Your first step toward authentic forgiveness must start with your accepting the grace and goodness of God, by asking Christ to come in and save you. He will make you a new creature, born again to the glory of God. For more information about this, turn to Appendix A right now!

But before we discuss what true forgiveness is, we must first look intently at some of our misconceptions. We must understand what forgiveness is *not*, because some of these misunderstandings are destroying our marriages.

Forgiveness Is Not Forgetting

Yes, Scripture clearly says in Isaiah 43:25 that "I, even I, am he who blots out your transgressions, for my own sake, and remembers your sins no more." God through His awesome mercy and grace forgives us of our transgressions. He remembers them no more. Yet as people with limitations, we do not always have the ability to forget. We do, however, have the ability to choose how we will respond when confronted with the memory of a past hurt, pain, or sin.

Forgiveness is not forgetting, but forgiving is a choice. You can decide not to allow the enemy to keep you hostage to the things you can't forget. You do this by intentionally applying Philippians 4:8–9, which states, "Finally, brothers, whatever is true, whatever is noble, whatever is right, whatever is pure, whatever is lovely, whatever is admirable—if anything is excellent or praiseworthy—think about such things. Whatever you have learned or received or heard from me, or seen in me—put it into practice. And the God of peace will be with you." What an awesome verse, and what a challenge to apply. Replacing painful memories with the power of God's Word will provide great strength as you demonstrate forgiveness to those who need it. God can transform your mind as you fill it with the truths of His Word.

Forgiveness Is Not Automatic Reconciliation

Many have been taught that after we say, "I'm sorry," everything should go back to the way it was. The problem is that often we shouldn't want things to go back to the way they were. We should want change to take place as each person recognizes and repents of their own sin. Coming through conflict can leave couples changed for the better. Understand, reconciliation is not automatic.

Reconciliation is a process. It takes time to heal and move beyond the hurt. But make no mistake about it, God desires for you to forgive others, to reconcile, and move forward in freedom with Christ. Paul in his writing to the church at Philippi addressed his haunting past as a persecutor of the early church. In Philippians 3:7–14, Paul challenges us to throw off the past failures and run the race ahead. He calls us to forget what is behind and strain toward what is ahead, as we press toward the goal. What goal is he talking about? The answer is found in verses 10 and 11: "I want to know Christ and the power of his resurrection, and the fellowship of sharing in his sufferings, becoming like him in his death, and so, somehow, to attain to the resurrection from the dead."

These passages speak clearly of our call to forgiveness and reconciliation. We cannot fully know Christ and the power of His resurrection without first experiencing His forgiveness. As we accept God's forgiveness and forget what is behind us, we can strain forward to know Christ intimately. Then we're truly on the road to reconciliation. You must become like Him in His death. You must die to your selfish ways, your selfish desires, and your personal agendas. When you do this, resurrection takes place in your marriage, and reconciliation begins to move forward as you submit to knowing and trusting the power of God.

Friend, our God is a God of reconciliation. This was the purpose of His giving Jesus—to reconcile a lost and dying world. This could only happen through the gift of forgiveness He offers to all who will receive. Once you forgive others, then you can begin the journey of reconciliation.

Forgiveness Is Not For Your Spouse

You must forgive because God forgave you. Forgiveness isn't for the other person. It's for you. Remember Isaiah 43:25 again, where God says "I am He who blots out your transgressions, for my own sake." God forgave us for His own sake. It was a measure of His love. He loves us so very much, that it was for His own sake that He offered forgiveness, because of who He is, not who we are.

When we forgive those who hurt us, we are not doing this because they deserve it but because we have been forgiven. You are causing yourself great pain when you don't forgive. Do you realize that not forgiving someone is a sin? This disobedience to the commands of God causes the unforgiving heart great turmoil. It causes anxiety, bitterness, depression, and hatred. It can act as a deadly cancer, eating at the very core of your soul.

We have the privilege of speaking at marriage conferences all across the country. After one of our conferences on forgiveness, a woman who was obviously burdened came up to us. She explained to us that she had divorce papers sitting on her desk at home. She said that if something didn't drastically change over the next 24 hours, she was leaving her husband. She went on to tell us that she was experiencing an unforgiving heart. Her marriage had suffered years of neglect and emptiness between the two of them. There was no connection between them. Years of pain had taken its toll on her and her health.

At that moment, she looked at us and said, "Are you telling me that I have to forgive my husband for all the things he has done wrong and failed to do right?" Jena reached over and tenderly held her hand. "Yes, dear lady, you do. You may never hear the words, *I am sorry.* You may never hear the words, *Will you forgive me.* You certainly didn't deserve this, yet in the midst of it all, you must still forgive."

As we concluded, the woman's husband joined us and we witnessed right before our very eyes the forgiving power of God. Her husband became broken before us. He confessed to his sin in the marriage. As they sat in the pew and cried, God mended two hearts that day. A marriage was restored because two people understood that they were to forgive for themselves and not the other person, out of obedience to God.

So if forgiveness is not forgetting, and it is not automatic reconciliation, and it is not for the other person but for you, then what is authentic forgiveness?

Growth of Forgiveness

When we are the ones in need of forgiveness, we must first be willing to confess our sins. The Greek word for confess is *homologeo,* which means to declare, acknowledge, to agree with and profess. It means to promise. Confession of our sins—agreeing with God about our sinful behavior—is the first step toward forgiveness. We must do this first with God, and then with those we have sinned against. Our confession then births repentance.

Repentance (from the Greek word *metanoia*) means to have a change of mind, a change in the direction of your will. You are headed in one direction, but after repenting of your sins, you change direction and head the other way. True repentance always involves a changed life. Countless couples have told us—and we have said—"their words mean nothing to me anymore. I've heard it all before, but things just stay the same." Why is this? Is it because we are not truly repentant?

There is a difference between worldly sorrow and godly sorrow, and 2 Corinthians 7:10 speaks to this: "Godly sorrow brings repentance that leads to salvation and leaves no regret, but worldly sorrow brings death." It is godly sorrow that causes change in a person's life. Godly sorrow means you agree with God and you see your sin the way He sees it. It causes grief, mourning, and heaviness of heart until it is dealt with, repented of, and forgiven. Worldly sorrow is simply, "I'm sorry that I got caught." Worldly sorrow involves self-justification and making excuses for your behavior. It is the opposite of repentance because it does not involve change and sanctification. One continues in disobedience to God's Word, causing emotional and spiritual death.

Too many couples attempt to mend their marriage by dealing with it in worldly terms, which are void of true repentance. The more this occurs, and the same sins are repeated, the more untrusting a couple becomes. For true forgiveness to occur, we must ask for the cleansing power of God in our lives. As the psalmist begged in Psalm 51:10, "Create in me a pure heart, O God, and renew a steadfast spirit within me."

The Demands of Authentic Forgiveness

To be an authentic forgiver demands we make three critical choices when faced with the opportunity to forgive. God will certainly use situations and circumstances to convict and direct, but He will not force you to do the right thing. You have a free will to act in obedience or disobedience to God, and reap the fruit of your choices. Scripture is clear regarding the law of the harvest. You will reap what you sow. In fact, you will reap more than you sow. The Bible says if you sow the wind, you will reap the whirlwind. If you want to reap love, you must sow love. If you want to reap compassion, you must sow compassion. If you want to reap forgiveness, you must sow forgiveness. The choice is yours. We learned in our reconciliation and remarriage that we cannot force one another to do anything. We have to make choices for ourselves and allow God to work in our spouse.

The Hebrew word for forgive is *aphiemi*. It means to send away; to bid going away or depart; of a husband divorcing his wife; to send forth; yield up; to let go; to disregard; and keep no longer. In other words, when sin enters your relationship, to be an authentic forgiver means you will no longer keep hold of the sin that separates you as a couple. In other words: *you are willing to accept the consequences of the other person's action, and not hold it against them.* As we studied the meaning of this word, we found it odd that the Strong's Study Guide referenced "of a husband divorcing his wife." This didn't sound like forgiveness to us, much less a proper application of the word. But as we pondered the intent and the very meaning, we realized this is exactly what happens when a divorce becomes a reality in a relationship. You bid your spouse to go away, depart from you—you disregard them and keep them no longer.

We did that to one another. We had become so emotionally distant that we began to operate as if the other one did not even exist. We had complete disregard for each other's feelings, and just wanted to get away from each other. Yet, in forgiveness, we are not to divorce ourselves from one another but from the sin that has taken up residence in our relationship. When a couple changes their focus from divorcing themselves from one another to divorcing themselves from the sin that separates, then they will be living and demonstrating authentic forgiveness.

Forgive As Christ Forgives

The first demand of an authentic forgiver is to **choose to forgive as Christ forgives.** In Matthew 6:12–15, Jesus teaches us to pray this way: "Forgive us our debts, as we also have forgiven our debtors. And lead us not into temptation, but deliver us from the evil one. For if you forgive men when they sin against you, your heavenly Father will also forgive you. But if you do not forgive men their sins, your Father will not forgive your sins."

Christ is clearly speaking about forgiveness. There is no room for misunderstanding in these verses. They clearly ring out the call for a choice to forgive. Verse 14 makes a definitive statement of what happens when you do not forgive. Christ is saying, *How can you accept My forgiveness and not be willing to offer that same forgiveness to those who have sinned against you?* In other words, *you hypocrite!*

You are operating your life under a double standard. One standard of how you wish to be treated, the other how you treat those who have wronged you. Choosing to forgive as Christ forgives requires a state of brokenness, humility, and selflessness. Christ is sinless, blameless. He walked this world doing no wrong, while being wronged Himself. As He hung on the cross, He spoke the words, "Father, forgive them, for they know not what they do."

As you recognize your sin and God's forgiveness that has set you free from the penalties of that sin, you can't help but be thankful. And as you walk in freedom, no longer a slave, but righteous, you begin to graciously bestow that to others. We believe that an individual can forgive only after they understand the depths of how much they have been forgiven.

Often we sin and we abuse the grace of God by continuing to sin, with a warped view that God will always forgive. Paul, in his writings to the church at Rome (Romans 6:1–7), addresses the relationship between, sin, forgiveness, and grace. He asked if grace abounded so that sin could abound the more. His answer was "Absolutely not!" The very measure of grace and forgiveness you offer others will be the same measure you will receive.

Often our forgiveness is not authentic; it is a façade. We forgive *as long as I don't need to bring it up later for my benefit.* We forgive with strings attached, hidden agendas, and impure motives. There is no grace in these facades of forgiveness, because you are forgiving on your terms, and not God's. It is fake, not authentic. Choosing to forgive as Christ forgives is forgiving completely. We must divorce the sin and hold onto it no longer. It is then that authentic forgiveness will become evident in your relationships. What a paradox. We must die to live, we must be buried to be raised, we must become a slave to be set free. When we make these choices, what we thought was dead becomes alive again.

Don't Bring It Up Again

The second demand of authentic forgiveness is that you **choose to not bring it up ever again**. This choice requires great discipline and self-control. Dale's mom speaks of the "bury the hatchet" principle. Many people in relationship live by this principle, whereby you say, "Let's just bury the hatchet!" The problem is that some people bury the hatchet with the handle down, and some people bury the hatchet with the handle up. Those who bury it with the handle up have already decided to go back and pick up the hatchet the next time a conflict arises, so they can do more damage. When this happens, the issue will rise again to divide the relationship.

Remember what we learned in Chapter Six? Love does not keep a record of wrong. It does not exhume the past sin once it has been forgiven. Aren't you glad that Christ does not bring up all your past sins? His forgiveness is genuine and does not keep a record of wrong. We understand that the application of this principle is not easy. The battle between our faith and our feelings is real.

As we walked through our days of reconciliation, this element of authentic forgiveness was not easily developed. The enemy loves to attack our minds. He comes with all kinds of accusations and doubts, keeping us hostage by bringing up the past. While we know that we should not do so, our flesh rises up and takes control of our behavior.

When we walked away from our "knee-to-knee" session, after we confessed our wrongs to one another, we were forgiving and forgiven. Yet three weeks later, the enemy attacked my (Jena's) thoughts and mind. When Dale arrived home, I let the bitterness take over. I said, "Dale, I cannot believe you let those people get on a witness stand and say all those hateful things about me! How could you do that?" Dale looked at me and replied, "Jena, I thought you forgave me for that!" I was instantly reminded of this element of authentic forgiveness: *You choose to not bring it up ever again.*

Now did bringing up the offense mean that I did not forgive Dale? Did it mean that authentic forgiveness did not occur back in the knee-to-knee counseling session? In our case, no! It simply meant that I made the wrong choice that day. We all make wrong choices. We respond in wrong ways, and are faced once again with the need to forgive. When a sin has been forgiven, you must wage battle/war with your mind and choose not to dwell on it or bring it up again.

The Bible helps us learn how to do this. In 2 Corinthians 10:4–6 we learn: "The weapons we fight with are not the weapons of the world. On the contrary, they have divine power to demolish strongholds. We demolish arguments and every pretension that sets itself up against the knowledge of God, and we take captive every thought to make it obedient to Christ. And we will be ready to punish every act of disobedience, once your obedience is complete."

When life attacks, pressure rises, and moments of conflict and disagreement occur, if you have more of Jesus Christ in your life and less of you, then what flows forth will be a choice to forgive. When we learned to authentically forgive in this manner, we were covenanted together never to speak again of the sin that we had committed against one another. The only exception to this covenant was for the edification, the building up, of those facing the same issues and struggles that we faced. That's why we have written this book, asking God to use our real life experiences to provide help and hope for someone else.

Take Initiative to Forgive

The third demand of an authentic forgiver is to **choose to forgive before forgiveness is ever needed**. This issue of forgiveness will not go away. It is not a matter of *if* but *when* the call to forgive will surface. You will be let down, you will be sinned against, hurt, and disappointed. Because these things are givens in relationships, we must choose

today to forgive tomorrow. Christ demonstrated this example during the very last days of His ministry here on earth.
John 13 describes Christ's decision to forgive before
forgiveness was ever needed.

Verse 1 says that, "Jesus knew that the time had come
for him to leave this world and go to the Father." The
Scripture says, "Having loved his own who were in the
world, he now showed them the full extent of his love."
His love was not merely verbal, but was also demonstrated
physically as He washed the disciples' feet. He humbled
Himself before those He loved. One by one, He washed the
feet of His disciples.

Whose feet did He wash that night? Judas Iscariot, who
was about to betray Jesus to His death. Peter, who would
that night deny three times that he even knew Jesus.
Thomas, who a few days later would doubt whether Christ
was indeed risen. He washed the other disciples' feet as
well—beloved friends who would fall asleep when He
asked them to keep watch. Jesus knew what was coming.
In washing their feet, Jesus was offering forgiveness before
it was ever needed. What an awesome display of love. If we
will learn to love like Christ, humbling ourselves before
one another, our marriages will be different.

Why love like this? John 13 provides us the answer, as
Jesus asks the disciples if they understand what He has
done for them. "Now that I, your Lord and Teacher, have
washed your feet . . . I have set you an example that you
should do as I have done for you. . . . Now that you know

these things, you will be blessed if you do them" (John 13:14–15,17).

People will betray you, deny you, reject you, and doubt you. It is not a matter of if but when. For our relationships to prosper and grow, moving beyond the sin and straining toward wholeness, we have to follow the example of Christ. We must practice authentic forgiveness. Maybe you feel like you didn't do anything wrong, or that the one who wronged you should be washing *your* feet. Remember that Jesus Christ, perfect in every way, got on His knees and washed others' feet. Could it be that our relationships will thrive only when we stop punishing others and become foot washers?

We have learned that we are not capable. We are weak and sinful and void of ability. Anything good in us is not us, but rather the supernatural power of God living inside of us. The moment we allowed Christ to take the throne of our lives, His power began to transform our minds. It transformed our relationship, and it transformed the way we viewed forgiveness. The divine power of God gives us all the courage and strength to forgive as Christ forgives, to choose not to bring it up ever again, and to forgive before forgiveness is needed. When this becomes a reality, an authentic Christ-centered relationship begins to grow and flourish into what God's original design was intended to become.

Chapter Nine

Spiritual Union

After Jena and I began to understand the truths that have been expressed in the preceding pages, we realized that there were some areas in our marriage that were missing. We learned about building safety in our home, releasing strongholds in our lives, demonstrating love and forgiveness, we even learned about finding our completeness in the person of Christ. But we still wondered if we were missing something.

Do you feel that way? Have you ever looked at others' marriages and thought, "They just seem to have something we don't. There is just something missing in our lives that makes us feel incomplete, but I can't put my finger on it. What it is, I just don't know!"

Well, we didn't know either. What did we miss the first eight years of our marriage? Did we even know what we were looking for? Jena and I didn't know that we had settled for second best. We bought a lie from the world, and it showed in our home. We poured our energy into the wrong areas. We only connected as a couple in small portions, instead of building a life together.

I poured my energy into being a good provider, protector, leader, and decision-maker. Having a sexual relationship with Jena was sure to connect us intimately, I thought. Yet for Jena, the focus was on the emotional and spiritual side of the relationship. This is the case for many marriages today. Husbands think they have a great marriage if they have great sex. Wives consider the marriage great if there is an emotional connection. They want to know the depths of their husband's heart. Men use sex to connect emotionally with their wives, while women use their emotions to connect sexually with their husbands. Very rarely does the couple connect spiritually. This was the case for us. The result: an incomplete marriage. With this realization, we began our search for God's picture of a complete marriage.

What we found is that marriage is not about complacency and co-existence. It's intended to be the ultimate relationship, created by God for deep, life-changing connection. We missed it. The Scripture is clear: God desires for husbands and wives to connect spiritually. He has a plan for this connection, and has provided for us the way in which to do so. In a complete marriage, the husband and wife develop a spiritual connection first.

Hopefully, by now, the Spirit of God has opened up the eyes of your heart so that you can see, know, and trust that the Lord is good. It is our prayer that you have learned something about yourself, and how your obedience and cooperation with Christ can strengthen your marriage. Most importantly, we pray that you have learned about the hope you have in Christ.

We are confident that God will help you take all the pieces of your journey and place them together so that you will indeed connect or re-connect to your spouse. Second best does not have to be a reality for you any longer. In order for your marriage to become the complete marriage God desires, you must learn to connect spiritually. We found that 1 Thessalonians 5:23–24 helped us understand how we can have a complete marriage.

"May God himself, the God of peace, sanctify you through and through. May your whole spirit, soul and body be kept blameless at the coming of our Lord Jesus Christ. The one who calls you is faithful and He will do it."

The truth is this: a marriage will only be as complete as the individuals are complete. Countless couples attempt to fix, change, and improve their marriage by fixing, changing, and improving their spouse. Yet we know from our own experience that the more we as individuals were transformed and became complete in Christ, the more our marriage was transformed and made complete by Christ. So, let's pick apart 1 Thessalonians 5:23 and see what we find.

Peace

First, God desires for peace to be evident in your marriage. Verse 23 calls God "the God of peace." When Christ, the Prince of Peace, came to earth, He came to bring us peace, and longs for couples to be at peace with one another. When was the last time you described your marriage as one of peace? We live in a world of busyness and selfishness, where there is little hope of peace. Yet God desires us to have peace. In Philippians 4:6, Paul plainly tells us to not worry about anything but to bring it to God and He will give us peace that will keep our minds and hearts set on Him. Isaiah 26:3 says, "You [God] will keep in perfect peace him whose mind is steadfast, because he trusts in you." When we lay our worries at His feet and keep our hearts and minds focused on Christ, He promises a peace that we cannot even understand (Proverbs 3:5–6).

Sanctification

God also desires for you and your marriage to be sanctified, to be holy. The Greek word for sanctify is *hagiazo*, meaning "to consecrate things to God, to separate from profane things, and dedicate to God." There should be a noticeable difference in your life, because of the difference Christ has made in you. This difference should show up in your marriage. You and your marriage are sanctified, set apart, dedicated to God for His good work. When someone looks at you and your marriage, they should witness something that God has sanctified. Perhaps it's time for you as a couple to dedicate your marriage to God, afresh and anew.

A Complete Marriage

After our re-marriage, Jena and I reflected on our first eight years of marriage, which ended in divorce. We intently focused on our lack of spiritual connection. We had been busy doing "churchy" things, deeply involved in the various ministry opportunities before us. Yet as a couple, we shared very little in the spiritual union God wanted us to experience. We didn't pray together, we didn't read the Scriptures together, nor did we discuss what God was doing in our lives as individuals. We didn't know what each other's favorite verses were, and why. Nor did we discuss what our passions were for God, and what we felt God was calling us to do with our lives. There were very few moments in our first eight years of marriage where we experienced a spiritual connection.

This is the testimony of far too many couples today. The epidemic of divorce in this country is due to the lack of spiritual union between a husband and a wife. Too many couples have settled for second best in the spiritual relationship with their spouses. The mentality is that praying together over dinner, attending the same Sunday school class, and even serving with great passion within the church somehow constitute having a spiritual marriage. Yes, these things are important, but if a couple is not intimately walking with God as individuals first, then together, they are not connecting spiritually as God designed. The external appearance of a spiritual partnership is evident, yet the internal reality of our hearts is that there is no connection.

Once again, the enemy had us hostage to lies that kept us from being connected spiritually. For me the lies were, "Don't pray with Jena—what if you pray wrong?" "Don't talk to her about God's Word—she knows the Bible better than you do anyway!" "Who do you think you are any-way—don't you remember that sin you just committed?" "It's okay not to talk with her about God—your spiritual life is private, just between you and God. You don't need to share it with her!" Lie after lie attacked the spiritual ele-ment in our marriage, as the enemy sought to steal, kill, and destroy this possibility for us. The truth we now fully understand is that God desires for a couple to develop a spiritual relationship long before anything else. It is only when a couple allows the Spirit of God to lead their lives and their marriage that they will experience a life-long, lasting love.

Jena didn't care what my prayers sounded like, she just wanted to pray with me. She didn't care which Scripture passage we read; she just wanted to be in the Word together. And the more that I kept her on the outside look-ing in, keeping the spiritual union at a distance between us, the more the enemy divided our home. The facts are simple: without a spiritual connection between a husband and a wife, a couple cannot have a complete marriage. Suc-cessful marriages are those where couples read the Word of God together, pray together, go to church together, walk with God together, communicating and connecting through the leading of the Holy Spirit.

The depth of spiritual connection between a husband and a wife is the source of power behind true intimacy and passion. It sounds so simple, yet it is the one area in which most couples struggle the most.

Here's how Jena and I jump-started our spiritual intimacy. We began to take small steps to pray together. We would each take a yellow post-it note and number the note 1, 2, 3. At the top of the note we would write, "How can I pray for you?" and ask each other to fill out three prayer requests. When we were back together that night, we had an immediate opportunity to discuss the reason for the three prayer requests, and how they had been answered. Instant spiritual intimacy was launched. We then moved to discussing what each other's favorite verse, passage of Scripture, and Christian hymn or song were, and why. We became intentional about finding out what each other's passions for God really were, and how we could be a source of encouragement in these areas.

It takes determination to build spiritual intimacy in marriage. Yet the blessings God desires to bestow upon you and your spouse will truly transform your marriage into the image of God. Once spiritual intimacy began to develop, we learned that we were connecting in other areas as well. We were experiencing emotional intimacy in our souls. This grew us toward true physical intimacy as a result. We began to discuss what we thought about spiritual matters, as well as matters that we faced every day.

Physical Intimacy

As we walked through our divorce and re-marriage, God transformed our understanding of physical intimacy. While the world would attempt to tell you that physical intimacy is the first thing to master to make a marriage successful, we have learned it to be one of the last. In fact, many couples today, just as we did the first eight years of marriage, are experiencing pseudo-intimacy. They are settling for second best when God has so much more in store for marriages. Understand, sex is not intimacy. If it were, the US would be the most intimate nation in the world.

We have learned that the more we become spiritually connected to Christ, the more we become spiritually connected to each other. The more we become spiritually connected to each other, the more our souls and hearts melt toward true intimacy. The more our hearts melt toward true intimacy in spirit and soul, the natural progression is to join together in true sexual intimacy.

We want to be very clear that a complete marriage does not mean that a couple is to be enmeshed in such a way that they no longer exist apart from one another. God's Word makes it very clear that we are responsible for ourselves alone. Our salvation and relationship with Christ is our own. We cannot piggyback to heaven on our spouse's back. We are individuals who are choosing life with Christ in a partnership, yet each party is responsible for himself.

A complete marriage does mean that you are connecting in spirit, soul and body, journeying through life together.

True Intimacy

Once Jena and I grew in our spiritual connection enough to begin those discussions, we learned to discuss other matters together through inquiring about each other's days. We talked about what we thought about issues at work and church, and with friends and family. We talked about what we thought of how our children were progressing in school, and if they were growing up into the people God wants them to be.

As our hearts listened and received one another's thoughts on various matters, we progressed into our feelings. Our hearts began to receive how we felt about all kinds of issues. Not just sterile, stale thoughts, but emotions and passion. Jena and I were beginning to develop true intimacy.

This was very evident during a doctor's visit I had. I found a knot on my side, which concerned both of us. Jena waited in the waiting room for 45 minutes while I was being examined. After the examination, Jena asked me, "Dale, what did the doctor say?" I replied, "He said he wants me to come back!" This answer did not provide connection, much less intimacy. Inside Jena's question there were more questions she wanted to have answered! She also wanted to connect emotionally. She wanted to know how I felt about all that was going on. Was I afraid? Could it be cancer? Would this require surgery? She wanted to know what was going on inside not just my head, but my heart. Conversation about simple facts must be accompanied with feelings so that a couple can connect in their souls.

Date Night

As our marriage grew, Jena and I discussed the spiritual things of God, what we thought about various issues, and how we felt about them as well. We then journeyed toward spending more one-on-one, non-sexual time together. Sharing your thoughts with one another is great, putting emotion and feelings with them is even better, but the entire soul connection of intimacy is held together as a couple spends concentrated, non-sexual time together. We want to encourage you to have a "date night." The hectic schedules that face the family today have driven a wedge between couples in this area of intimacy. At a very minimum, a couple should have one night a month where they spend time together, just the two of them.

Developing some social time with your spouse does not mean that you call up your closest friends and go to dinner and a movie. The reality of this is that during dinner, the women sit and talk together, while the men do the same. You then get to the movie and no one talks to anyone. You go home thinking you had a great night together as a couple, while in actuality you may have had fun, but no depth was added to your soul connection. This is not to say that getting together with friends is not important or valuable. The point here is that a couple needs to spend some one-on-one time together, connecting in their mind, wills, and emotions, leading them to deeper levels of intimacy.

I was leading a men's conference several years ago, and I asked the men in attendance to grade themselves on the spiritual and the soul connection in their marriages. I asked them to rate themselves on a scale of 1–5 with 5 being the highest, and 1 being the lowest. As I asked, "Men, where do you grade yourself in the area of spiritual intimacy with your wives?" The men began to call out their scores, "I'm a 2, I'm a 1, I'm a 3!" I then asked "Where are you in sharing your thoughts, your feelings, your heart, and spending one-on-one, non-sexual time with your wives?" Again, the same answers, with similar scores. But when I asked them to respond to their sexual intimacy, the room roared as man after man yelled "4!" "5!" and "Hey, I'm a 10!" I responded, "I know we have a room full of *studs*, but if your wife thinks you're a *thud*, who do you think is going to win this test?"

A complete marriage is not something that just happens one day. It requires daily dedication and commitment. Marriages include moments of great exhilaration and ecstasy, as well as moments of enduring together. The good news is that the plan and path that God has for us can be full of abundance and joy no matter what comes our way.

The more that we strive to develop a complete marriage, the more we will experience what the God of peace sanctified and set us apart for.

A Marriage Restored

For us, it became very simple. God brought us to a crucifixion moment in our lives. We came face to face with our faith, questioning if we were really willing to trust God and His Word. If we were, then it required one thing from us— obedience. We had to obey God and His commands for us as individuals. We had to begin to live with integrity, honesty, purity of heart and motive. We had to let God have control. We had to take our hopeless state and place it in the hands of Christ.

Look at Revelation 2: 4–5: "Yet I hold this against you: You have forsaken your first love. Remember the height from which you have fallen! Repent and do the things you did at first. If you do not repent, I will come to you and remove your lamp stand from its place."

This Scripture provided us with the pathway to re-connecting. We first had to repent of the sin that had separated our intimacy. We then remembered the good things about our relationship. We remembered the times that we cherished together, and the days of joy and happiness. We were compelled to envision how far we had truly fallen. The wonderful memories of our relationship, combined with the brokenness of how far our sin had taken us, made us fall on our faces, fully dependent upon God.

When you are flat on your back with no place to look but heavenward, God steps in. As we repented, and remembered, we repeated. We put back into practice the things we used to do to nourish and nurture our relationship. We began acting like we loved each other. We repeated the small things we used to do. We started dating each other again. We began serving one another, not to manipulate for our own personal agenda, but as true ministers. We learned that the "little things" really do mean a lot. As time carried us from our past and focused us on our future, we fell back in love.

How is it possible? Because God is faithful and true to His word. He is a God of hope. 1 Thessalonians 5:24 provided us the promise: "The one who calls you is faithful and he will do it." God had revealed Himself in mighty ways as we walked our road of reconciliation. While we may not have known it at the time, the still small voice of God was calling us. He so desired for us to walk with Him, hear His voice, and trust His heart.

God is calling you as well. He is calling you back into a right relationship with Him. He is also calling you to become a safe mate, to minister not manipulate, to love, and to forgive. He is calling you to let go of your pride and selfish desires, and lay down the sword of contention, picking up the sword of His Word to protect your home from the advances of the enemy. He is calling you to humility and commitment. He is calling you to obedience.

The good news is this: He is faithful.

We can testify from our own experiences that this is true. God never let us down. He is true to His Word and to His promises. He is faithful to the end and He will accomplish it for you as you yield yourself to Him. You have only one response: "Yes Lord! We will trust and obey." You've heard it said, "It takes two. Two to make it, and two to break it!" We would tell you it takes three: two willing partners, and Jesus Christ. We pray you will start today on your journey toward a complete marriage, saying, "Yes, Lord," every step of the way.

Chapter Ten

The Fragrance
of Christ

I f you have journeyed to the end of this book, you have proven one thing: that you desire to seek wholeness in your relationship with Christ and with your spouse. If you are a child of God, then your ultimate pursuit is holiness, a life set apart for His glory. And your desire for holiness is not for your glory, but for God alone. As you strive for holiness, you will receive wholeness in Christ. But in order for both holiness and wholeness to develop within you, you must learn to embrace the brokenness that is required to do so.

Many of you understand brokenness. Some truths within this book may have brought you to your knees over the mistakes you have made in your journey with Christ and in your marriage. God wants your broken heart to bring you into deeper fellowship with Him. He wants to continue His refining work in your life. He desires your holiness too, so that you will accurately represent Him in the world.

But let's face it. The thought of embracing brokenness is not very appealing in and of itself. Quite frankly, none of us enjoy or desire brokenness. We would be content and happy to never experience those growing pains. And that is just it. If we never experienced brokenness, we would be content just as we are and never grow and go with God. It is through the broken times that God draws us unto Himself and continues His good work that He began in us and is faithful to complete (Philippians 1:6).

When we went through the brokenness of our marriage, neither of us embraced brokenness at all. As a matter of fact, we fought God tooth and nail, like a horse fighting his master's bridle. We had no desire to allow our Master to tame us or bring us into submission to His authority.

Psalm 51:17 says this, "The sacrifices of God are a broken spirit; a broken and contrite heart, O God, you will not despise." The word "contrite" means "to crush like powder." When we went through the devastation of our divorce, we were brought to the end of ourselves, literally with our hearts crushed like powder before God. Our lives were nothing but broken pieces. But God's work was not complete. He restored our marriage with a purpose in mind.

One day after Dale and I reconciled, Dale was riding in the car, listening to a CD by the Christian musician Clay Crosse. As he worshipped and communed with God, the song "Stained Glass Window" (by Mark Heimermann and Phil Madeira) began to play. Some of the words to the song are:

Just beneath the rafters, in a church of stone,
Lay a stained glass window in the attic all alone.
A work of art forgotten, a treasure thrown away.
Taken from the sunlight, it was just a useless frame.

Oh, the things in life we take for granted
Oh, the things of wonder we could know
Oh, I want to be illuminated
Full of Heaven's light, shining through my life
Let the window of my heart reveal Your love.

With every word of the song, Dale encountered God's calling to ministry. He quickly called me and we together confirmed God's calling on our lives to minister to families in what is now called Stained Glass Ministries.

Our marriage had been shattered, ruined beyond all repair, we thought. But God picked us up, cleaned us up, and put the broken pieces of our lives back together again. Then as we allowed the light of His Son, Jesus Christ, to shine through, what a beautiful stained glass marriage He created.

As we embarked on our ministry voyage, the Lord convicted us about our children. We did not want to remarry only to travel and leave them behind. So to encourage them to embrace our ministry instead of resenting it, we called a family meeting and shared God's call for our family. We shared with them that this was not Dale and Jena's ministry, but God's ministry through our family. We helped them understand that they were a part of this, too. Both

Cole and Jorja have joined us whole-heartedly in ministry through singing, running our slides, selling products, and sacrificially serving alongside of us. It is the joy of our hearts to see our children loving and serving the body of Christ.

As we began writing this book, our children began to pray diligently for us. One day, Cole told us that he had something he had written to children and that he wanted in the book. This is what we believe God inspired our son to write:

Hi, I am Cole Forehand.

My parents are the writers of this book that your
    parents are reading.

When I was 7 years old, my parents got a divorce.

These were some things I did:

When I was afraid, I hid behind couches and chairs.

When I was angry, I yelled at them.

I even remember tearing up all of my dad's business
    cards one day.

My dad said, "Cole what are you doing?"

I said, " Daddy, I am mad at you for divorcing my
    mommy."

These were some things I felt:

sad, mad, scared, and freaked out.

I thought it was my fault, but it wasn't.

Look, just understand that they love you the same
    together or apart.

If you don't know God the right way, pray this with me:
"Dear God, I don't want to be empty inside any more.
   Come into my heart. Amen."
You can e-mail me at my mom and dad's web site if you
   need a friend.

—Cole Forehand

Moms and dads, husbands and wives, God truly does provide hope for hurting families. Our children, Cole and Jorja, were instrumental in helping us come face to face with the reality of divorce and the effect it had on them. The world we live in glamorizes divorce. It paints a distorted picture of what divorce does to family members.

But brokenness can be a wonderful thing, when handed to God. God loves to take broken things and use them for His glory. God used many people in the Bible, just like you, after they were broken. We believe that He does this to give no room for question or speculation as to who should receive the glory. It is all about His grace and His goodness. If your marriage seems to be shattered, with no hope for repair, there is hope for you in the person of Jesus Christ. He will lift you up, change you from the inside out, and then allow you to encourage and help another along life's journey.

Paul understood this well as he penned, "Praise be to the God and Father of our Lord Jesus Christ, the Father of compassion and the God of all comfort, who comforts us in all our troubles, so that we can comfort those in any trouble with the comfort we ourselves have received from

God" (2 Corinthians 1:3–4). Paul could embrace broken-ness because of the hope that he would be able one day to help another who traveled a similar path.

In the book of Joshua, we see a journey to brokenness that offers hope for us today. As the book begins, Moses has just died and Joshua has been appointed by God to lead the children of Israel into the land of promise. Joshua believed God and followed Him with all his heart. As the Lord led Joshua to conquer Jericho, Joshua told the people not to take any spoil from the city, because it would bring trouble upon them from the Lord. But one person, Achan, chose not to believe these words. Coveting the treasures of Jericho, he took some things, causing the anger of the Lord to burn against all Israel. (Our sin does affect more people than just us.)

Therefore, as they approached the city of Ai, which means "ruin," and attempted to overcome their adversaries, the Lord allowed them to be defeated at a place called She-barim, which means, "broken." Joshua 7:5 says, "The hearts of the people melted and became like water."

Have you reached the place called "broken"? Do you feel that your life or marriage is in utter ruin? When our marriage crumbled in defeat, we realized firsthand that our sin as individuals and as a couple had brought us to this very place.

The cities of Ai and Shebarim are located in central Palestine. Do you know what plant grows in Palestine? Myrrh. The significance of this plant is vital. Myrrh was one of the gifts that the wise men brought to the baby Jesus

(Matthew 2:11), and myrrh was applied to Jesus' body after His death (John 19:39–40). Myrrh is a small shrub that grows in rocks and sand in Palestine. It produces a fragrance when it is injured or broken. As a matter of fact, the more it is broken, the more fragrant it becomes.

Oh, friend, do you see? When Jesus Christ was broken for you and me, He emitted a sweet fragrance for the world to breathe, through His unending, never-changing love. Likewise, when we find ourselves broken and ruined, it is then that we should totally depend upon Him. Through your broken dependence, you become a beautiful fragrance of Jesus Christ. "But thanks be to God, who always leads us in triumph in Christ, and manifests through us the sweet aroma of the knowledge of Him in every place. For we are a fragrance of Christ" (2 Corinthians 2:14–15*a* NASB).

God can take the broken pieces of your life, clean them up, and put them back together again. If your marriage seems to be shattered, with no hope for repair, there is hope for you in the person of Jesus Christ. He will lift you up, change you, and put your life together in a new and beautiful way.

So choose your journey's end. Allow God to write your story. Ephesians 2:10 says, "For we are God's workmanship, created in Christ Jesus to do good works, which God prepared in advance for us to do." Let God begin His work of holiness in your marriage. As your holiness leads to wholeness, He will unfold His unique plan for you to share your story. There's a lost and dying world that desperately needs to know the hope you've found in Jesus Christ. He's given you a story, so be ready to tell it for His glory.

God is still in the business of doing miracles. It may not be water into wine, but He is saving marriages, providing hope, and changing lives. And there is no greater miracle than a changed life. May God richly bless you as you strive to know Him more and honor Him with your life and your marriage.

"May our Lord Jesus Christ himself and God our Father, who loved us and by his grace gave us eternal encouragement and good hope, encourage your hearts and strengthen you in every good deed and word."
—2 Thessalonians 2:16–17

Appendix

How to Become A Christian

This section may be the most important one you read in this entire book. Everything else that is written will not compare to what God will do through your life as you surrender to Him. No marriage will ever reach the heights unless both partners are born again. As you read below, follow the five steps to salvation and accept Jesus as your Lord. After your decision to follow Christ, you will never to be the same again. May God transform you into the person He desires for you to be as you allow Jesus to become the Savior of your soul and the Lord of your life.

Step 1: Recognize That God Loves You

"For God so loved the world that he gave his one and only Son, that whoever believes in him shall not perish but have eternal life" (John 3:16).

Step 2: Recognize That You Have Sinned

"For all have sinned and fall short of the glory of God" (Romans 3:23).

Step 3: Recognize That Sin's Debt Must Be Paid

"For the wages of sin is death, but the gift of God is eternal life in Christ Jesus our Lord" (Romans 6:23).

Step 4: Recognize That Christ Paid for Your Sins

"But God demonstrates his own love for us in this: While we were still sinners, Christ died for us" (Romans 5:8).

Step 5: Pray and Receive Christ Today

"Everyone who calls on the name of the Lord will be saved" (Romans 10:13).

"For he says, 'In the time of my favor I heard you, and in the day of salvation I helped you.' I tell you, now is the time of God's favor, now is the day of salvation" (2 Corinthians 6:2).

Today, you can receive Christ as your Lord and Savior. As you agree with the Scriptures above, simply pray this prayer in your heart:

"Dear Jesus, I invite You to forgive me of my sins and come into my heart and life right now. I accept the payment of my sins by the shed blood of Christ. I accept You, Jesus, as my Lord and Savior. Please reveal Yourself to me and become real in my life from this moment. Thank You for saving me and giving me eternal life. I love You and commit my life to You. Amen."

What To Do Now?

We want to encourage you to do the following three things as a response to your decision.

1. Tell someone. Tell a close friend, your spouse, even tell us. We would love to hear from you.

2. Find a church home that will baptize you and nurture you in your new walk with the Lord.

3. Commit to grow daily in your new Christian life by reading the Bible, praying, and having fellowship with other believers.